3. 3. 74

Continental China Collecting
for Amateurs

Also by J. P. Cushion:

ENGLISH CHINA COLLECTING FOR AMATEURS

J. P. Cushion

Continental China
Collecting for Amateurs

FREDERICK MULLER

*First published in Great Britain 1970
by Frederick Muller Ltd., Fleet Street, London, E.C.4*

Copyright © 1970 J. P. Cushion

*Printed in Great Britain
by Ebenezer Baylis and Son Ltd.
The Trinity Press, Worcester, and London
Bound by Wm. Brendon and Son Ltd.*

SBN: 584 10051 5

1797608

CONTENTS

ILLUSTRATIONS

Introduction

The previous volume in this collectors' series dealing with pottery and porcelain covered the popular wares produced in the British Isles. This new volume covers the many types of pottery and porcelain made on the Continent, particularly those wares most frequently encountered by collectors in Britain.

There is little doubt that of the many examples of decorative art collected today the most popular are those made from varying forms of fired clay. In this field, probably more than any other, it is possible to collect according to the purchaser's means: for some the precious, and often rare, productions of China, Germany, France or England, but for many the more humble domestic earthenwares which can often be purchased for a few shillings and yet give equal pleasure if tastefully displayed in a suitable setting.

The field covered by decorative ceramic wares produced in Europe during the past five hundred years is vast and, as with English wares, requires constant visits to museums and major sale-rooms to familiarize the intending collector with the range of productions and enable him to quickly recognize materials, techniques, palettes and styles.

At all levels the most successful collectors are those who, having first gained a good background knowledge, proceed to concentrate their attention upon the wares of one country, type or factory and so become specialists in this particular field. Such collectors are often able to quickly spot a rare example; while dealers and museum curators have to endeavour to cover the entire range of antiques.

The most popular and well-known wares made on the Continent have, of course, been more widely reproduced than those made in England. There are few people who have not heard of such factories as Dresden, Sèvres, Capodimonte or Limoges, all famous factories or centres of manufactures bearing marks now well-known and easily recognized, although sometimes wrongly associated with an earlier factory. These are the wares which, since the nineteenth century, manufacturers or decorators have profitably imitated or reproduced, copying in some cases not only the style but also the mark associated with that factory. Whereas in other cases a popular style of decoration associated with a famous factory was adopted together with a mark, deliberately designed to confuse the buyer. In this respect the famous "crossed-sword" mark, adopted in 1723, is without doubt the most plagiarized. Weesp (Holland) and Tournay (Belgium) both used similar "crossed-swords", but with interspersed dots or crosses respectively; the Paris factory of La Courtille used crossed "torches", Rauenstein (Thuringia, Germany), crossed "hooks", Rudolstadt, from the same area, crossed "hayforks". The Meissen-like devices met most frequently are, however, those used by the mid-nineteenth-century Thuringian manufacturers Alfred Voigt of Sitzendorf and Schierholz and Son of Plaue-on-Havel: the first, two strokes with a third drawn across; the second, two strokes crossed with a further two, a real "double-cross".

While the majority of the porcelains produced in Germany have nearly always been of hard-paste (or true porcelain), those made in France until about 1770 were of soft-paste (or artificial porcelain), an exception worth noting being the Strasbourg hard-paste porcelain of Paul Hannong (1752–55). Fortunately most people concerned with reproducing "early Sèvres" in the nineteenth century seem to have been unaware of these differences of material, consequently making it all too easy for the collector to recognize many fakes. No piece of hard-paste porcelain with a Sèvres mark should have a date letter indicating a year of manufacture prior to 1768 (P) at the very earliest (see p. 168).

Records concerning the majority of the great Continental porcelain factories are usually fairly complete and have, in most instances been published in monographs dealing with the one particular factory, thus knowledge of marks, styles of decorators and modellers, together with dates of their employment, should all be utilized in an attempt toward making a correct attribution. Unfortunately this is not always the case with many of the earlier and sometimes humbler earthenwares, and collectors must therefore rely upon documented examples in public collections.

The various tin-glazed earthenwares of Spain, Italy, Holland and France have been popular with collectors from the times such wares were first produced by the Arab-invaders of the Iberian Peninsula from about the beginning of the twelfth century. The manufacture of similar metallic-lustred wares continues in the province of Valencia to the present day, but bear little resemblance to the original masterpieces, as does the productions of the traditional forms of tin-glazed wares— known as maiolica, Delftware, and faience in their respective countries, and many a new collector, if not well acquainted with the original wares, can make a bad buy.

The earthenwares made by small provincial factories or individual potters can at times prove confusing. To produce porcelain it is necessary to have expensive equipment and a good technical knowledge, whereas with earthenwares the most humble potter can sometimes produce quite remarkable and often baffling examples. Many are the times I have suspected some unusual piece of pottery as having been produced only a week or two previously at the local evening institute pottery-class!

Among the many wares that are enjoying popularity today are the German salt-glazed stonewares. These often present posers, especially if they have been made following traditional sixteenth-century forms. Stonewares very rarely reveal any signs of age—the hard, "orange-peel" textured glaze cannot be "dressed-up" with seemingly age-old scratches so often to be seen on lead-glazed bodies. On many pieces of French faience good evidence appears in the form of parallel-lines made by a metal file, revealing the hand of a rogue.

Factory-marks are of course notoriously widely faked, especially those applied in enamel colour or gilding on top of glaze; therefore trying to correctly attribute a piece of pottery or porcelain, I suggest the mark, if any, should be the last detail examined; apart from finally verifying the attribution, it is very satisfying to ones ego to find that the mark exactly confirms the diagnosis made on other evidence. The first stop should be to check basic material, or body: is it earthenware, or porcelain? Although this is usually obvious, there are many wares that call for the simple check on translucency: when most porcelains are held before a strong light, unless the piece has been exceptionally heavily potted or underfired, a certain amount of translucency (i.e. light appearing through the body) is apparent. Secondly, is the material hard-paste porcelain, as discovered by the Chinese over a thousand years ago, or one of the artificial pastes as used in the early factories of France? Is the glaze a lead-glaze or feldspathic as made from china-stone, has it been made opaque with tin-oxide, as in "delft-ware", or is it a white clay slip under a lead-glaze? Are the colours used in the decoration of early date, or does the palette contain the familiar pinks and greens derived from chrome that have only become available since the early nineteenth century?

The answers to such questions and many others are dealt with under the respective countries; first the earthenwares and stonewares, secondly the porcelains.

Part I

Materials and Techniques

Earthenware, stoneware and the various types of porcelain are all composed of different clays, nearly all of which require a certain amount of preparation and possibly the addition of chemicals before the desired body and finish are achieved.

The early wares of the fourteenth and fifteenth centuries had very little in the way of refinement. Pots were "thrown" by the local potter from clay found in the immediate locality, and were then often decorated with a coating of clay, usually of a light colour. Generally known as "slip" (any type of ceramic clay when watered down to a creamy consistency is termed "slip"), this further wash of clay was applied to the body of the vessel while it was still "cheese" or "leather" hard, that is, it still contained some moisture and consequently had not started to shrink to any great degree.

Another technical term which will often be used in discussions concerning pottery and porcelain is "biscuit". The term "in" or "on the biscuit" simply refers to the condition of the clay body after the first kiln firing, where the plastic clay is changed to a hard brittle material. Most wares go through further kiln firings to receive underglaze colours, glaze, enamel decorations or gilding. Some porcelain figures such as those made at Vincennes and Sèvres were deliberately left "in the biscuit" to imitate marble statuary.

Earthenwares made from local clays vary from dark reds to creamy whites. Such bodies, even when fired in the potters' kilns at temperatures ranging from between 1,000°C–1,200°C, remain porous and consequently cannot be used to hold liquids over a long period. Thus glazing soon became a necessity as a watertight barrier for vessels for purposes other than the storage of dry materials or the cooling of the contents by evaporation. Taking the form of a thin layer of glass, the technique of glazing was probably first practised in Egypt or Mesopotamia at least as early as the ninth century B.C.; these early glazes made from quartz sand and soda (siliceous glaze), were prone to decay if buried, often resulting in the much-admired iridescence of so many early wares. Since about 300 B.C., lead-glaze was frequently used on earthenwares. Formed by either pouncing the vessel with powdered lead galena or dipping it into a bath of liquid glaze (as described under Maiolica), the lead oxide combined with the natural silicates in the clay when fired to form a glass-like glaze.

We are all probably familiar with stoneware, though not always recognizing it as such. The light-grey marmalade pots, old ginger-beer bottles, much laboratory equipment, even the large drainage pipes regularly inserted into road excavations, are all forms of salt-glazed stoneware. This particular body is richer in natural "fluxes" than earthenware, that is, it contains a certain amount of felspar, so that when fired to between 1,200°C–1,250°C the material vitrifies and becomes a solid mass. Receptacles of this material can thus be used to hold liquids without the further addition of a glaze. In order to make these wares more hygienic and pleasant to handle, salt (sodium chloride) was shovelled into the kiln at the peak firing temperature, and the sodium combined with the clay silicates to form a thin, hard film with a texture usually likened to orange-peel. Sometimes, in order to produce a rich brown or blue finish, as on some German stonewares, the body was brushed or painted with a slip containing iron-oxide or cobalt.

Later a similar but very much more refined body fired at a lower temperature and covered with a fine lead-glaze rather yellowish in colour, resulted in the well-known cream-coloured earthenware as perfected by Josiah Wedgwood by 1765. This was the material which became so popular throughout Europe (known in France as *faïence fine*), that the majority of potters engaged in the making of maiolica, faience or Delft-ware, were forced to abandon their old technique of applying an opaque tin-glaze to low-fired earthenware, and began to imitate the highly popular Queen's ware of Wedgwood.

East led the Western world in the making of true porcelain by about eight hundred years, although there were some minor attempts resulting in the production of various "soft-paste" porcelains from the late-sixteenth century in Florence. By the ninth century the Chinese had discovered the two essential materials, china-clay (kaolin) and china-stone (petuntse), and were producing a fine, white, translucent material from these two forms of decomposed granite mixed with a fluxing agent; the glaze was composed of china-stone together with such fluxing agents as lime and potash. The Chinese aptly described kaolin and petuntse as the skeleton and the flesh of porcelain; the non-fusible china-clay providing the white skeleton around which the translucent "flesh" of the china-stone was fused. They tended to use a greater proportion of china-stone in their mixture than the later European potters, with the result that their kiln temperatures were only about 1,350°C as compared with the 1,400°C of such factories as Meissen; consequently the Chinese wares are usually a little softer and not quite so white. Their firing techniques further differed from those later employed in Europe in that they preferred to apply glaze to the wares before the initial "biscuit" firing, thus combining the firing of body and glaze. The

European porcelain potter first fired the body to a low temperature, then applied the glaze by either dipping or spraying, and
finally fired the piece at the full high temperature. In both
cases, of course, the glaze formed a water-resisting layer over
the body, only occasionally "crazing" (a minute crackling of
the glaze).

It was not until 1710 that the Meissen factory was established in Saxony for the production of white hard-paste
porcelain; since about 1708 they had been making a very fine,
hard red stoneware. Similar hard-paste porcelain was made
from 1719 at Vienna and in Venice from 1720, the majority of
other well-known German factories not commencing production until about the middle of the eighteenth century.

The earliest attempts at imitating the much-admired
Chinese wares were, to our knowledge, first made in Florence
from about 1575. This was a soft-paste porcelain composed of
a mixture of white firing clay and the ingredients of glass which
had been fused and powdered (called frit). This type of
porcelain only required a temperature of about 1,100°C, but
was much more difficult to form into a shape, was less plastic,
often warped in the kiln, and was subject to cracking with
sudden changes of temperature. The glazing of soft-paste
porcelain always called for a second firing, the glaze being composed of lead-glass; this thin layer of glaze did not always fit
the body as well as that on hard-paste porcelain and was more
subject to crazing.

Those who have seen a potter "throwing" at a wheel will
know that he first centres his prepared material, and gradually
draws up the clay to form a basic chimney-pot shape from
which he is able to fashion almost any circular form desired.
Obviously not all forms and shapes can be made in this way
and consequently moulds are necessary to give shape to the
moist clay and then support it while it is drying out. A
modeller first prepared the shape of the hollow-ware or figure

in wax, alabaster, plaster or wood and this master copy had to be made oversize to allow for the shrinkage of the clay in the initial "biscuit-firing". When completed, the model was handed over to the mould-maker who was responsible for preparing the plaster-mould. Moulding can be carried out in two different ways, in the case of "press-moulding" the prepared sheets of clay were pressed into the inner walls of the mould by hand and the various sections subsequently sealed along the seams with slip, or a process known as "slip-casting" was used. This process involved pouring the prepared slip into the hollow assembled moulds. The dry plaster immediately started to absorb the water from the slip, thus building up a layer of clay on the internal walls of the mould; when through long experience, the potter knew the clay to be of the required thickness, the remaining slip was poured out. In about fifteen minutes the mould could be opened, and the thin-walled, hollow reproduction of the original model could be removed. Most hollow-wares could be produced in a simple two-part mould, possibly requiring the addition of a slip-cast pouring spout and a press-moulded (solid) handle.

Figures with a large amount of under-cutting necessitated the dividing of the original model into several convenient pieces which were then moulded separately. To make up a complicated group such as a centrepiece, the skill of a "repairer" was required. It was the job of this craftsman to assemble the various moulded pieces while they were still "cheese-hard", attaching them with slip. Although he followed a completed standard model, the arms, heads and legs of figures from the same moulds were often unintentionally made up in slightly different poses. Often reproductions of earlier figures have been revealed as such through their being smaller than known genuine pieces; the copies were made from moulds taken from an original figure and consequently further shrinkage has occurred.

Many of the relief patterns around the borders of Continental porcelain plates were incorporated in the moulds on to which discs of clay were pressed, the reverse and foot-rim then being shaped on the wheel while the clay was still on the mould.

The natural colours of various clays were considered sufficient as decoration for early pottery, especially when covered with the thick lead-glaze; use was often made of such metallic oxides as copper or manganese which applied together with the lead galena resulted in a moss-green or purplish-brown coloured glaze. The practice of employing a glaze which was clear until made white and opaque through the addition of tin-oxide again originated in the Near East, at first used for glazing tiles, and in the ninth century A.D. to enhance the appearance of pots. Lead-glazes were very fluid when fired, so that decoration was apt to be blurred, whereas one advantage of tin-glazing was that it was very stable and rarely "ran"; in addition the white ground was ideal for decoration. Knowledge of this technique spread from the Near-East across Europe, being first seen on the Hispano-Moresque wares of Spain, and successively in the "maiolica" of Italy, the "faience" of France, the "Fayence" of Germany, and the "Delftware" of Holland, all usual alternative names for an identical process. The "high-temperature colours" were painted on to the highly-absorbent surface of the glaze before firing, thus giving the decorator no opportunity to erase mistakes or alter his composition apart from washing off the entire coating of unfired glaze from the biscuit and starting afresh. It is on Italian maiolica of the late fifteenth century that the full range of "high-temperature" colours available are seen to best advantage. Here, in addition to the two metallic oxides of copper and manganese just mentioned, are to be seen blues made from cobalt, yellow from antimony, orange from iron-rust, and blacks made from a mixture of these colours.

Of exceptional interest are the very fine lustre colours

found on Hispano-Moresque wares and the Italian wares made at Gubbio and Deruta. These copper and yellow colours with a mother-of-pearl iridescence were particularly difficult to achieve, and called for special treatment and kiln conditions in a third firing. Use of silver oxide resulted in the well-known brassy yellow, whilst copper was used to obtain the rich ruby lustre. When fired in a low-temperature kiln in which burning green wood created dense smoke, a thin film of metal was left fused to the glaze; a small amount of polishing gave the desired effect. Such pieces were sometimes given a second, clear lead-glaze which added further brilliance to the colours. Prior to the nineteenth century, blue and red and a rare manganese, were the only colours which could be successfully fired together with the glaze of porcelain, the technique having been practised by the Chinese since at least the early fourteenth century. Blue from cobalt was quite common and could be fired under almost any kiln conditions as an underglaze-colour painted directly onto the body of the porcelain, over which the glaze was applied and the two were fired together. Underglaze copper-red is much less common as it was a colour requiring very precise kiln conditions and temperatures. It was not until the second quarter of the nineteenth century that improved knowledge of chemistry made possible such underglaze colours as pinks, greens and yellows.

The full range of colours normally used in the decoration of porcelain and pottery are enamel colours, derived from further metallic oxides. These were applied on top of the glaze to which they were fused in what is known as a "muffle-kiln" at a temperature of approximately 800°C. It should be noted that in the case of soft-paste porcelain the bright colours have been partially muted by absorption into the glaze, whereas colours tend to lie clearly on the surface of the glaze of hard-paste porcelain and at times even flake off.

If gold were to be added to decorated pottery or porcelain a fourth firing was necessary, the ground-up gold powder or leaf having been mixed with one of several media before application. Usually honey was used, but later in the eighteenth century an amalgam of gold and mercury was preferred, giving a brighter metallic result. After application as a pigment, the gold was fixed in a low-firing kiln and subsequently burnished with a bloodstone or agate. Interesting contrasts have sometimes been obtained on some of the expensive wares made since the nineteenth century by the application of gilding to a glaze which has been acid-etched with a pattern, the high-relief gilding is then burnished, leaving the sunken areas of the design in the yellow matt gold.

A decorating technique first introduced in England and only rarely used on Continental wares, is transfer-printing. In this process a skilled craftsman first engraved a copper-plate with a design to the required scale of the object to be decorated. His work was sometimes original, but more often engravings from well-known pictures or earlier publications were copied. The enamel pigment which would normally have been used by the artist, was then rubbed into the engraved design and the surplus colour was wiped from the plain surface. A thin sheet of paper was then carefully spread upon the copper-plate and pressed down into close contact. When the paper was removed the pigment from the engraved design was taken up on the underside. The enamel pattern was then carefully placed into position on the glazed surface of the pottery or porcelain, the paper was then soaked off and the piece was ready for the muffle-kiln for fixing. Very little use was made of this method on Continental wares, the exceptions being such places as Marieberg in Sweden, Zürich and later cream-wares of such places as Montereau, Creil and Choisy-le-Roy in France.

Part II

Pottery

Spain

Twelfth-century Spain may well be considered the converging point of Eastern and Western pottery styles for in A.D. 711 the Arabs invaded the Iberian Peninsula, and by at least the beginning of the thirteenth century had started manufacturing tin-glazed earthenwares (generally termed "Hispano-Moresque" today); dishes and vases of this ware were often further decorated with the metallic lustre of copper or silver, a technique that had been practised in the Near East since the ninth century.

It is from the Arabic geographer Edrisi, writing of Calatayud in 1154 that we first learn that here "the gold-coloured pottery is made which is exported to all countries". Further evidence of the manufacture of similar wares in the mid-fourteenth century is given by the traveller, Ibn Batutah who wrote, "At Malaga the fine golden pottery is made which is exported to the furthermost countries"; later writings sing the praises of "the beauty of the gold pottery so splendidly painted at Manises", near Valencia (Pl. 1A).

The manufacture of these lustre-decorated wares called for far greater accuracy of kiln conditions than those required for normal tin-glazing with high-temperature blue (cobalt) decoration. The technique employed in both Spain and Italy necessitated firing the piece to the biscuit state, over which the opaque white glaze was applied and the piece again fired. The lustre pigment, whether copper or silver, was then administered with either a brush or quill-pen. A third firing in a kiln using such fuel as damp brushwood or rosemary to acquire the necessary smoky atmosphere produced the carbon, which in turn united with the oxygen in the pigment. This resulted in a layer of pure reduced metal being partially absorbed into the glaze with the lustrous "mother-of-pearl" finish so admired at the time.

Existing specimens of the early wares of the fifteenth and sixteenth centuries are now mostly to be found in museums and famous collections, and are consequently difficult to acquire except by extreme luck. The most common shapes are dishes and tall waisted jars made for the apothecaries and decorated in one of about ten popular styles. These early wares often feature lines of meaningless mock-Arabic script, but serve to remind one of the fact that such pottery had its beginnings in the lands of Islam. Many of these more important pieces were further decorated with the arms of the owner thus forming good evidence of the style of a particular period, such as the large pan-shaped charger in the Victoria and Albert Museum which displays the arms of Mary, Consort of Alfonso V of Aragon, thus giving a date of between 1415 and 1458. A further popular early style employed at Valencia was the decoration of the entire ground surrounding a central coat-of-arms with five- or six-petalled flowers having thin encircling stems on a dotted ground, a fashion copied on the early Italian wares produced at Faenza, where similar use was made of the vine and bryony leaf Manises designs.

The high quality of these early wares continued well into the sixteenth century, but there is a noticeable decline in quality towards 1650 when much of the skill shown by the Moorish potters appears to have been lost; the fine pale greenish-tinged gold giving way to a deep, metallic copper of a distinct reddish hue. A further guide to the recognition of early wares is the high quality of decoration often to be found upon reversing large dishes which in many cases surpasses that upon the face. While not decrying such draughtsmanship, it is necessary to recall that the decorator was, of course, painting on a smooth fired ground and not on the difficult unfired tin-glaze.

As with all popular collectors' items, there are many pitfalls for the newcomer, and such wares as these (for which vast sums were paid in Victorian days), have been reproduced for many years at Manises, not far from the city of Valencia. This centre makes all manner of pottery and tiles, some in the styles of early Seville and Talavera, but their speciality is the traditional lustre for which the centre was famous. Here again the present-day bright copper-lustre lacks the iridescence seen upon original pieces.

A further ceramic industry undoubtedly introduced into Spain by Arab potters was concerned with the manufacture of tiles (*azulejos*). Evidence of the early technique of piecing together in a mosaic pattern, simple shapes cut from glazed and fired slabs of earthenware, into large sections which were then applied to the wall, can be seen at the palace of the Alhambra, in Granada. These tile designs are datable to the fourteenth century, but the practice of decorating walls in this manner does not seem to have spread far beyond the province of Andalusia.

This laborious method of achieving a clear-cut division between the different coloured glazes was the only one known at the time, but during the second half of the fifteenth century the so-called *cuerda seca* (dry-cord) technique was adopted to prevent the coloured glazes mingling. This practice consisted of drawing the outline of the chosen pattern onto the tile in a greasy substance coloured to a deep purple, which formed a barrier keeping the coloured glazes in position during the firing. Early in the sixteenth century Seville and Toledo set the fashion for moulded tiles; the soft earthenware was stamped with a mould which left a design in the form of thin raised walls of clay and these compartments were then flooded with colour and fired. (A technique which could well have been suggested by Chinese *cloisonné*.)

The pottery centre of Paterna near Valencia has been rather overshadowed by Manises. Its earliest wares probably date from the fourteenth century, being painted in manganese and copper on a white tin-glazed ground and are often confused with Italian wares made at Orvieto. Plant-forms, foliage, animals, birds, figures and heads were all very much in the Islamic manner, but the similarity in treatment of the wares attributed to this centre suggests a rather short span of life: from about 1350–1450.

Since the fifteenth century Talavera had been making white and green glazed vessels in the manner of the wares made at Toledo, but from the sixteenth century developed styles which quickly became popular throughout the country. Once again we are reminded of the favour found by many tin-glazed wares among the doctoring fraternity, for in 1575 King Philip II gave 359 pieces to the Escorial Monastery, many of which were drug-jars. Many of the decorated wares were painted in fashionable Italian styles, and were obviously destined for the palaces of the wealthy.

The style of painting most readily identified with Talavera is that decorated in a peasant-like fashion with birds, animals or busts, in blue and dirty-orange, outlined with purplish-black; while only dark-blue was used on the coarser wares which were often painted with such figures as birds, deer or rabbits, serving as a reminder that hunting was the most popular sport of the day (Pl. 1A).

Wares produced at Talavera continued to be acceptable to

all levels of Spanish society into the seventeenth century, on a scale comparable to the creamwares of Wedgwood in England during the succeeding century. Many pieces painted with monastic coats-of-arms and the familiar cardinal's hat also continued to be produced, but were now decorated with the yellow, orange and green associated with this centre. The same colours were used on much grander bowls and two-handled jars to depict sporting scenes, bullfights, buildings, trees, figures and animals.

It was not until the mid-eighteenth century that Talavera potters abandoned their traditional styles and shapes for more fashionable styles made popular at Alcora in the Province of Valencia, which in turn was directly copying the French wares of Moustiers. Painting such delicate Bérain-style designs on an unfired tin-glaze called for a skill to which the Talavera potters were rarely accustomed, and so the often very blurred painting looks rather crude when compared with the original Alcora wares.

Knowledge of pottery and porcelain made at Alcora in the eighteenth century is very complete. The factory was first established in 1726 by Count Aranda, and within a year pottery was being made "in the manner of China, Holland and other localities". The man responsible for this immediate success was Joseph Olerys, a painter who had previously worked at Marseilles, and was eventually to return to Moustiers in 1739. The tin-glazed pottery made at Alcora was popular throughout Spain and the Count's manufactory was granted many privileges, such as freedom of custom-house duties.

Although the original success of the factory was due to the skill of French painters and the use of French models, by 1737 the entire personnel was Spanish. The output was enormous and the standard of workmanship of the highest quality. Letters to the Tribunal of Commerce tell of "pyramids with figures of children, holding garlands of flowers and baskets of fruits on their heads" and "three-cornered tables, large objects, some as large as five feet high, to be placed upon them, chandeliers, cornucopias, statues of different kinds and animals of different sorts and sizes".

The absence of any regular factory-mark on Alcora faience makes the certain attribution of many pieces decorated in the Moustiers fashion extremely difficult; the Spanish diaper-borders and pendant decoration do, however, tend to be a little more fussy than the French. The most original painting attributed to Alcora took the form of biblical or mythological scenes on either large dishes or moulded picture-like plaques; many of these paintings in high-temperature colours closely rival some of the best Italian pictorial examples. Apart from the distinctly reddish clay body, the surest guide to a correct attribution of Alcora faience is the recognition of the high-temperature colours; orange, purplish-black and strong-greens with occasional use of the now-familiar copper-lustre as used at Manises, colours that should never be confused with the softer tones of Moustiers.

On the death of the founder in 1749 the manufactory passed into the possession of his son and later to successive Dukes of Hija until 1858 when it was acquired by private owners; after this few wares of a decorative nature were produced.

The popularity of Wedgwood's cream-coloured earthenware throughout Europe made it necessary for the factory at Alcora to produce a similar body. In 1774 François Martin was engaged to produce "hard-paste porcelain, Japanese faience, English paste (pipeclay), and likewise to mould and bake it". Wedgwood, however, had little to fear from this new competition, for although nearly all his most popular bodies were reproduced, it is only the cream-coloured figures, sometimes modelled by Julian Lopez, which deserve mention (the porcelains of Alcora are discussed in Part III).

A traditional form of coarse pottery which has changed very

bove (Pl. 1A), spouted vase, tin-glazed earthenware (*maiolica*), decorated with high-temperature ~~ours. Italian (Urbino), *c.* 1580. Ht: 11½ in.; dish, tin-glazed earthenware, painted in blue, ~~rple and orange. Spanish (Talavera), 17th century. Diam: 14⅛ in.; jug, tin-glazed earthen-~~re, with lustre decoration. Spanish (Valencia), *c.* 1600–25. Ht: 10 in. *Below* (Pl. 1B), plate, ~~-glazed earthenware painted in enamel colours. Italian (Faenza, Ferniani factory), 1750–60. ~~am: 9⅜ in.; vase, tin-glazed earthenware, painted in blue. Italian (Savona), late 17th century. ~~ : 9 in.; plaque, tin-glazed earthenware painted in high-temperature colours. Italian (Castelli, factory of Dr. F. A. S. Grue), 1686–1746. Diam: 9⅜ in.

Above (Pl. 2A), vase, blue tin-glazed earthenware, painted in white and yellow. French (Never, second half of 17th century. Ht: 7¼ in.; plate, tin-glazed earthenware, painted in blue and re French (Rouen), early 18th century. Diam: 9⅜ in.; porringer and cover, tin-glazed earthenwa painted in blue, yellow and green. Mark, 'OL' monogram. French (Moustiers), *c.* 1740– W.: 5¼ in. *Below* (Pl. 2B), plate, tin-glazed earthenware, painted in enamel colours. Fren (Lunéville), mid-19th century. Diam: 9⅜ in.; pot-pourri, tin-glazed earthenware, painted enamel colours. Mark, monogram 'JH' in blue. French (Strasburg, J. Hannong), *c.* 1770. H 9⅛ in.; plate, tin-glazed earthenware, painted in enamel colours. Mark, monogram 'VP' in gre French (Marseilles, Veuve Perrin), *c.* 1770. Diam: 9¾ in.

little since the early sixteenth century is that of the unglazed earthenware pitchers or *bucaros*; these vessels kept their contents cool by evaporation through the porous body and can still be seen in use by the Spanish farm-labourer or road-repairer.

Portugal

The most noteworthy contribution the potters of Portugal have made towards European decorative ceramics is seen in their fine quality tin-glazed tiles of the sixteenth century. During the seventeenth century the Portuguese, through their trade with the Far East, became conversant with the vast quantities of blue-and-white porcelain being exported from China, with the result that they produced some very fine examples of maiolica decorated in high-temperature blue in the Ming style. Such wares were made at either Lisbon or Braga and consisted chiefly of dishes (following silver shapes), vases, bottles, ewers and the popular drug-jars.

Among the many eighteenth century factories in Portugal making faience in later Italian styles, the most noteworthy was that started at Rato in 1767. The "F.R./TB" (in monogram) for Thomas Brunetto or "F.R./A" for Sebastiao de Almeida are sometimes seen on silver-form table-wares painted in the Turin or Savona manner.

The Portuguese factory with which new collectors are most likely to become acquainted was established in 1853 by Mafra & Son at Caldas da Rainha; this concern has specialized in making easily identifiable reproductions of the more grotesque Bernard Palissy wares (see p. 60. Pl. 6A).

Italy

We have already read of the early tin-glazed earthenwares made in Spain; the so-called Hispano-Moresque wares. Such wares undoubtedly found their way into Italy, and we are told that the actual term "maiolica" was adopted in Italy through the importation of the Spanish wares by the trading ships from the Balearic island of Majorca. For many years Italian maiolicas have featured prominently in great collections, and in the 1784 catalogue of Horace Walpole's Strawberry Hill collection we find entries recording "Raphael faience" and "Raffaelle ware", which was thought to be due to the fact that many such pieces were painted after prints of the original works of that great artist.

The documented records concerning the early manufacture of Italian maiolica are probably better than those of any other ware. In about 1558 Cipriano Piccolpasso of Castel Durante produced a manuscript account of the entire production techniques illustrated with wood-engravings. In this he tells of the preparation of the clay, the building and firing of the kilns, glazing and painting methods and of how special pieces received a second clear glaze (*coperta*) to give an extra fine finish.

Probably the first large Italian pottery centre to make an early type of maiolica was at Orvieto in Umbria. Most of the pieces attributed to this place are dated around 1400, but having been excavated, and consequently discoloured, they are rarely seen at their best. They can, in addition, almost be classed as peasant pottery since the forms, though practical, are clumsy, and where the white-glaze does not cover the foot-rim the clay appears much browner and harder than the later and preferable, soft biscuit-colour body as employed elsewhere. The palette consisted of two major colours; green from copper, and purple from manganese. It was used to produce some very good stylized bird painting in the Near Eastern manner, showing a similar treatment of the background; the decorator seemed loath to leave any space empty and preferred to fill in with Gothic-like foliage and cross-hatching. This feature is not seen on similar wares made at Paterna in Spain.

The Florentine wares made around the middle of the fifteenth century are of two distinct types; the easiest to identify being the large drug-pots made for hospitals and often bearing the badge of some establishment. In shape they are bold and practical having two strap handles and painted in a blackish-blue outlined in dark-purple. The decoration usually consisted of fine heraldic beasts, upon a ground painted with stylized oak-leaves, which gives the name "oak-leaf" jars to the entire group. The second early Florentine group were obviously intended for display upon sideboards; as they mainly consist of large pan-shaped dishes painted in purple, green, yellow and blue. The centre is usually decorated with the image of a human head or an animal, while the surrounding wall and rim are covered with bold curling leaves.

It is not always possible to relate certain styles of Italian maiolica to factories in specific cities in the same way as the pottery wares made elsewhere. The roving habits of many Italian potters are sometimes recorded in the inscriptions on the backs of many dishes; these give the name of the potter, his birthplace or normal place of work and where he was when painting the particular example.

Maiolica is really seen at its best from the first half of the sixteenth century when highly skilled decorators employed its surface much as an artist would a canvas. With the introduction of Renaissance styles came more ambitious figural subjects, encircled by foliage and employing the full range of high-temperature colours.

From the late fourteenth century the city of Faenza, situated between Bologna and Rimini, had been associated with the manufacture of maiolica and from the mid-fifteenth century a style was developed there which enables more confident attributions than are possible with many other areas of production. Together with the usual large drug-pots some very fine baluster-shaped vases were produced, being decorated with heraldic devices, figures in contemporary clothing and typical Gothic foliage, with a ground or wide-band of peacock-feather ornament coupled with ivy or bryony floral swirls, which was also mentioned as appearing on Spanish wares. In nearly all cases the palette is dominated by a very strong deep-blue. On the majority of these late fifteenth-century wares great use was made of the still very Gothic foliage to fill the spaces surrounding the main subject-matter, a practice referred to as "contouring". The few documented wares produced at Faenza during this period serve as key indications to the forms, style and palette in vogue at a precise date. There is, for example, the service made for Matthias Corvinus, King of Hungary, at the time of his second marriage in 1476 to Beatrice of Naples.

During the second half of the fifteenth century the Faenza potters made a number of large pieces in full relief which were probably inspired by the Florentine enamelled *terra-cottas* produced at the Della Robbia workshops; these took the form of Nativity groups, fountains, mirror-holders and inkstands.

Factory-marks can rarely be associated with maiolica potteries of the early period, although an exception exists in the case of the early sixteenth-century Casa Pirota at Faenza, the workshop of the Pirotti family, who adopted as their mark a circle quartered by a cross with a small circle in one segment. It is on marked dishes and plates from this factory that the first painted historical and religious scenes appear. A further decorative style especially associated with the Casa Pirota is that known as a *berettino*. Here the tin-glazed ground was stained blue, and designs such as symmetrical grotesques were then painted on the ground in opaque-white. This manner of painting was particularly preferred as a border design by a Casa Pirota painter generally known as "The Green Man"; as he also had a preference for using several varying shades of green in his designs.

The full signature of a potter or painter is only rarely seen on fifteenth-century maiolica, but by the second quarter of the sixteenth century the full names of some Faenza potters do appear; one name sometimes seen is that of Baldassare Manara, whose dishes have pleasing decorative patterns on the reverse side.

By the middle of the sixteenth century several well-known Faenza painters were engaged in painting in the style particularly associated with the wares made at Urbino: the entire front surface of the dish is taken up with figure subjects, a fashion referred to as *istoriato*. Furthermore the Faenza potters at this time appear to have become more conversant with Far Eastern porcelain, for between about 1550 and 1650 they developed a popular style called *bianchi di Faenza*, depending on the minimum of decoration (generally a few *putti*) on the white tin-glaze.

In 1693 Count Annibale Ferniani acquired an existing Faenza pottery and produced both tiles and table-wares. The factory continued until at least the early part of this century and many wares made from about this period are often to be seen painted in imitation of Japanese Arita porcelain or French faience.

During the third quarter of the eighteenth century use was made of the full range of enamel colours which were applied to the white fired glaze, imitating the Chinese porcelain painted in the *famille rose* palette (Pl. 1B).

It should also be noted that during the sixteenth century maiolica was also made at Ravenna and Forli in the neighbourhood of Faenza. These wares are, however, very rare and their attribution is still disputed by specialists.

Cafaggiolo, near Florence, was the seat of the younger branch of the Medici family. The maiolica factory established here about 1506 lasted almost until the end of the century, remaining in the hands of the Fattorini family the whole time. Judging by the number of pieces attributed to this factory bearing heraldic devices and arms of the Medici, there is little doubt that the factory was mainly established with the aim of supplying the needs of the family. One outstanding painter signed himself "*Japo in Chafagguolo*" (Jacopo), and several very fine pieces in the collection of the Victoria and Albert Museum are attributed to this painter. This hand can often be identified by his characteristic method of painting the grassy foreground with tufts which often suggest large crabs or spiders.

Apart from the large numbers of fine dishes and plates which were obviously made for decorative purposes only there are a number of large practical jugs; very heavy, even when empty, these are usually boldly painted with the arms of a family or person of some note or high rank.

Pieces painted with grotesques, usually attributed to

Urbino, are known to date during the later years of the Cafaggiolo factory. (Pl. 1A).

Siena, in Tuscany, had a flourishing maiolica manufactory as early as the middle of the thirteenth century, but it was not until the early sixteenth century that its wares can be identified in any quantity. These are pieces often associated with Maestro Benedetto who, in about 1520, supplied a large number of apothecary pots to the Hospital of Santa Maria della Scala.

Apart from many dishes displaying biblical characters, Siena produced many paving tiles, some of which were originally made for the Petrucci Palace. These, in common with the decorative dishes, show a preference in the palette for an opaque dark orange colour.

The most notable contribution to eighteenth-century Sienese wares are the painted dishes and panels by Ferdinando Maria Campani and Bartolomeo Terchi, decorated in a style and palette more popularly associated with Castelli. In both cases buffs and light blues are very much in evidence, with Terchi also favouring a very dark brown.

From later in the fifteenth century until the present day Deruta in Umbria has had a large pottery industry. Here, in addition to wares painted in the usual range of high-temperature colours, many pieces with metallic lustre decoration were produced in the same manner as those discussed under Spanish wares. The late fifteenth-century dishes, painted in blue, orange and green and lacking the early purple derived from manganese, are again sometimes difficult to attribute with certainty. But they sometimes have one peculiar feature; to achieve a "near-flesh" tint the enamel is scraped away to reveal the pinkish-clay body, over which was then applied a clear lead-glaze.

The early sixteenth-century lustre of Deruta is a brassy-yellow outlined in a soft blue, showing, when correctly fired, a "mother-of-pearl" iridescence; later wares are deeper in tone, veering towards an olive-green. Most of the original pieces take the form of large dishes, with tin-glaze on the front only, and a colourless lead-glaze on the reverse. Occasionally, use was also made of moulds to produce dishes and small bowls with raised decoration, the deeper dishes often featuring a raised central boss, apparently to fit the base of a matching ewer.

Among the many very good reproductions made of Deruta lustre-ware are such pieces as that illustrated on Pl. 6B. This example was made at the Florentine workshop of Ulysse Cantagalli (d. 1901); production started in 1878 and reproductions were also made in the fashion of Urbino, Faenza, Gubbio and della Robbia. Since so many pieces bear his mark of a blue cockerel, it would seem likely that his copies were invariably marked, with no intention to defraud.

Famous for the "ruby-lustre" was the workshop at Gubbio in the duchy of Urbino. The skill of Maestro Giorgio (Giorgio Andreoli, d. 1553) and his family eventually became so admired that wares made at other centres were sent to Gubbio to be further enriched with the deep red lustre derived from copper. Maestro Giorgio specially introduced new shapes to show his lustres to advantage; albarellos with oblique gadroons, moulded dishes and covered cups with bosses were all used to reflect the brilliance of the ruby decoration. Documentary evidence proves that at Gubbio they were not only concerned with decorating other workshops' wares as was once suggested, but made pots themselves. It is, however, difficult at times to sort out the composite pieces from those both made and decorated at Gubbio.

The town of Castel Durante in the duchy of Urbino (renamed Urbania in 1635), is famous as the birthplace of two outstanding personalities concerned with maiolica, Nicola Pellipario and Cipriano Piccolpasso; the first thought of as the greatest master of maiolica painting, while the latter was the author of the manuscript, *Li tre libri dell' Arte del Vasaio* ("The three books of the Potter's Art").

The earliest wares made at Castel Durante can sometimes be attributed to a very accomplished painter and potter, Giovanni Maria, whose signature is recorded upon a dish dated 1508. This painter specialized in a highly accomplished style of painting "grotesque and trophy" borders around plates with deep wells containing beautifully drawn heads of youths or girls.

Nicola Pellipario was born about 1480 and appears to have moved away from Castel Durante by about 1527. On his earliest works can be seen the fully developed style of pictorial painting, first introduced by the painters at Faenza. In about 1519 he painted the well-known service of Isabella d'Este, wife of Gianfrancesco Gonzaga, the marquis of Mantua, in which every plate or dish had, in addition to heraldic arms, a different subject taken from classical mythology, such as Hippolytus and Phaedra or Apollo and Daphne. These compositions were sometimes original, but more often they were taken from woodcut illustrations of a slightly earlier date. In every case his own interpretation of the original work showed Pellipario to be a very outstanding artist in his own right.

Urbino, the capital city of the duchy, appears not to have been a maiolica centre until a workshop was established there by one "Guido da Castello Durante" in about 1520. Guido was the son of Nicola Pellipario and owed his success to the patronage of the della Rovere dukes. By about 1527 Nicola had migrated from Castel Durante to his son's workshop at Urbino, but his work was of a decidedly lower quality as he approached old age.

The Fontana workshop, established by the above Guido was responsible for many signed pieces, but where a signature is lacking it is often difficult to know whether a piece was painted by his father, himself or his son Orazio Fontana, who in 1565 started his own workshop adjacent to that of his father. There are in existence several wares painted with the name "ORAZIO" in monogram. Such large pieces as wine-coolers, salvers, vases, pilgrim-bottles and stands were made at the Fontana workshop and decorated in a style introduced and made popular by this workshop. The main feature of the decoration included graceful arabesques and grotesques painted in colour upon a white ground and edged with yellow picked out in orange; imitation antique cameos were often worked into the tracery (Pl. 1A). The inspiration for this style is undoubtedly to be found in the paintings of Raphael in the Loggie of the Vatican, which were in turn derived from ancient Roman frescoes. Toward the end of the sixteenth century the Patanazzi family workshop, also in Urbino, produced many models in the Fontana manner but of very inferior workmanship.

The painter whose work at Urbino is often easy to recognize is Francesco Xanto Avelli. His crowded scenes suggest a stage-setting and his characters, with their over-rounded limbs, his palette is predominated by bright yellows and orange. The majority of Xanto's pieces can be dated within the decade 1530–40.

There are probably many more recent imitations of the Urbino "arabesque-grotesque" style than of any other maiolica and these can usually be detected by the pen-like draughts-manship of the painting, suggesting that the white tin-glaze ground had first been fired to make painting easier. Even more noticeable is the inclusion of a pinkish-purple which was not available to the sixteenth-century painter.

From about 1540 maiolica painted in the *istoriato* style, as first popularized by Nicola Pellipario, was also made at Pesaro by Girolamo di Lanfranco and his son Giacomo; such pieces are, however, extremely rare. In this same area, during the third quarter of the eighteenth century, Antonio Casali and Filippo Caligari produced many practical wares such as drug-jars, lamps, food-warmers, jugs, cups and saucers. These pieces were painted in the later French fashion with low-fired enamel colours; crimson roses heavily out-lined in black, with bright green leaves, were a favourite pattern.

Although examples of the maiolica manufactured at Venice can be dated as early as 1520, production on a larger scale does not seem to have developed until the middle of the century. Since Venice was an important trading port, the Venetians were well acquainted with pottery from the Near East and porcelain from the Far East long before most other Europeans. The influence of such wares is obvious in their maiolicas, of which the ground colours are usually stained to a lavender-blue, and upon this the decoration is painted in a strong cobalt blue, with only a rare touch of opaque-white or yellow to emphasize a particular feature. Such European subjects as the "Labours of Hercules" are often coupled with graceful arabesques, obviously derived from Chinese export-porcelain of the Ming dynasty.

Maiolica potters worked in Padua, near Venice, from the fifteenth century onwards, and their tin-glazed wares were painted in the same palette as that used at Venice. There is, in addition, evidence of work in the *sgraffiato* technique. (See Bologna p. 47).

A class of Paduan ware which might well cause some confusion with Turkish pottery was made from about 1625–1700. The pieces were obviously copied directly from the sixteenth- and seventeenth-century wares made at Isnik. Stylized tulips, hyacinths, carnations, were all painted in a palette lacking only the outstanding "sealing-wax" red of the Near Eastern pottery; the brownish-orange employed in its stead is a very poor substitute.

Castelli, in the kingdom of Naples, is best known for the maiolica made in the town from the late seventeenth century by the Grue and Gentili families. Even at this late date no factory-marks appear to have been used, but frequent signatures permit comparatively accurate attributions to be made.

Carlo Antonio Grue (*d.* 1723) is considered as being responsible for the acknowledged Castelli style which is usually so rich in architectural details and borders with flowers and *putti*, painted in varying tones of buffs, pale yellows, and greenish-browns. His styles were continued by his sons, Francesco Antonio (*d.* 1746), and Anastasio (*d.* 1743), Aurelio (*d.* 1744) and Liborio (*d.* 1776). (Pl. 1B).

Maiolica was certainly made at various centres on the Ligurian coast since at least the sixteenth century, but these wares are rarely encountered by modest collectors. More frequently seen, however, are those made in the seventeenth and eighteenth centuries often having the mark of the arms of Savona or a crudely drawn lighthouse. Such later Savona pieces were rather heavily potted in a bold baroque style imitating contemporary silver forms (Pl. 1B); the decoration was usually in blue alone, the designs tending to follow the fashionable Ming porcelain. Occasionally the full range of high-temperature colours appears, but usually applied in a rather heavy handed manner, not unlike Talavera, depicting small detached scenes of such sporting animals as the hare amid foliage, and hounds.

Often seen on Savona wares is a "falcon", the mark of Sebastiano Folco who worked towards the end of the eighteenth century and favoured a speckled manganese ground with attractively painted tiny scenes in reserved panels, including figures, buildings, etc. Mention must also certainly be made of the Borelli family who were apparently engaged in producing tin-glazed earthenware in the Castelli style as early as 1735. The last known potter of this family is Giacomo Borelli who worked in the late-eighteenth and early-nineteenth century. He is known to have previously worked in Marseilles, and consequently his wares tend to follow the fashions of that French centre, but in a rather more crude form. Borelli is also known to have made figures: some painted, others left in the biscuit state, as well as a not un-attractive butter-coloured creamware with brick-red painted or printed decoration. (Also known as Boselli, Boselly or Borelli.)

During the seventeenth and eighteenth centuries there were many minor factories engaged in producing wares similar to those described above. Many of these factories eventually turned to the production of lead-glazed earthenware in the English, or Wedgwood style. The workshops of Turin, functioning since about 1650, produced both monochrome and polychrome wares in the Savona styles; the mark most frequently used was the shield of Savoy under a ducal crown. Giorgio Giacinto Rossetti, commencing in about 1737, preferred to imitate the styles of the French Moustiers factory and often marked pieces "TR" (Torino-Rossetti) or "GR" (Giorgio Rossetti). Rossetti's work is also recorded at the Lombardy factory of Lodi.

F.S   Milano   . 3
·C   F≠C   P R
                             Mil^no

In the middle of the eighteenth century there were two rival establishments in Milan. The factory of Felice Clerici lasted from 1745 until about 1780; his tin-glazed earthenwares show a preference for Chinese styles painted in high temperature polychrome. Pasquale Rubati established his factory in 1759 and chose to paint his wares with the greater range of low-fired enamel colours in imitation of such costly porcelains as Sèvres. In 1790 his son Carlo, who had succeeded his father, abandoned the production of tin-glazed wares in favour of the English style cream-ware.

Another late factory concerned with both earthenware and hard-paste porcelain was established at Nove, near Bassano, in 1728 by Giovanni Battista Antonibon, to be succeeded in turn by his son Pasquale (1738) and grandson Giovanni Battista (1762). The factory was leased to Giovanni Baroni in 1802 but later reverted to the Antonibon family, in whose hands it remained until late in the nineteenth century.

It was the Nove factory which was responsible for the well-known tureens in the form of fish, as well as practical Rococo form table-wares painted in high-temperature colours. The mark of a "star with a tail" is quite often seen on nineteenth-century wares.

Some very good quality cream-colour earthenware was made at Nove from about 1780 by Giovanni Maria Baccin, and a little later by such potters as Baroni, Bernardi, Viero and Cecchetto; in most cases easily identifiable by self-explanatory marks. The earliest, and most prolific, cream-ware manu-factory in Italy was the factory established in Naples in 1760 by Nicola Giustiniani and continued by his family throughout the nineteenth century. Apart from Wedgwood-type table-wares, many excellent figures were produced. The marks usually consist of impressed initials of the proprietor with "N" for Naples (Pl. 5B). Similar wares were also made from the late eighteenth century by Cherinto Vecchio and his son, marked "FDV/N", "del Vecchio/N", or "GDVN" for Gennaro de Vecchio Napoli.

Particularly associated with Padua and Bologna is an early and rare type of earthenware. These wares are referred to as *sgraffito* or *sgraffiato* as the result of the technique employed in their decoration. The body of these pieces was of red clay coated with a white slip, the design then being scratched through the top dressing to reveal the basic red. The whole was then covered with a distinctly yellow-toned lead-glaze often dappled with patches of green or golden-brown pigment. The majority of such pieces were made in about 1500 and are naturally very rare, but there exists a very dangerous class of reproductions made by Carlo Giano Loretz & Company of Milan. Bologna should also be noted as the city where Angelo Minghetti and Son are known to have made many excellent reproductions of Renaissance maiolica from 1849.

Germany, Austria and Central Europe

Some of the earliest forms of decorative pottery made in Germany were the wares of the *Hafner* or "stove-maker". These rare and important museum pieces are unlikely to come the way of the amateur collector, but they certainly merit mention. The manufacture of pottery stoves in Europe dates back to Roman times, but few can be attributed to a date earlier than about 1350. During the fifteenth century most of the tiles used to form these stoves were covered with a green lead-glaze and shaped in a concave manner to aid the radiation of the heat from the burning charcoal. This style of manufacture gave way in the following century to tiles made from yellow, brown and white clays, or tin-glazing over the light-red clay bodies. Such tiles were widely used in the sixteenth century for stoves in Germany, Austria and Switzerland, and without knowledge of their place of origin they are very difficult to correctly attribute.

Occasionally the stoneware producers made vessels, which are also referred to as *Hafner*-ware. Paul and Kunz Preuning of Nuremberg are particularly associated with a colourful version of these wares, produced during the middle decades of the sixteenth century. Probably inspired by the form of the earlier green-glazed Gothic stove-tiles, they often decorated their large jugs with recesses into which were placed figure-subjects in the round, coloured with the full palette offered by high-temperature oxides.

A further type of *Hafner*-ware was produced at Neisse, near Breslau in Silesia. The colourful wares were decorated with various coloured opaque tin-glazes kept apart during the firing by deep scratches or incisions made into the clay, giving an effect similar to that on the Spanish tiles made in the *cuerda seca* technique. Dated pieces range from mid-sixteenth century to the early seventeenth century and depict such subjects as the Crucifixion, Emperor Rudolph (1576–1612) and the arms of the Bishop of Breslau.

As we have already noted, stoneware is a highly fired body (c. 1200°C–1400°C), consequently we find that the manufacture of such wares in Europe was restricted to the Northern areas where plentiful supplies of wood were available to attain and retain kiln-temperatures.

Some of the finest German salt-glazed stoneware was produced in the Rhineland. Siegburg was an important centre from the fourteenth century until 1632, when the town was devastated by the Swedes. The fifteenth-century wares are of a near-white colour with only a very thin, colourless glaze, the most favoured shapes being the *Trichterbecher*, a cup with a funnel-shaped mouth, and the tall slender jugs. The cups were often decorated with various armorial and other devices applied in relief.

The Siegburg potters tended to copy the more elaborate fashions of Cologne from about 1550, and many tall tapering tankards (*Schnellen*) are to be seen with very high quality relief decorations attributed to F. Trac. Some interesting vessels were also made at Siegburg by Anno Knütgen and his family during the second half of the sixteenth century. These included very large jars fitted with candle-sockets, flasks in the form of a hollow-ring, and smaller jugs made to resemble owls.

The centre in Germany for Rhenish stoneware was at Cologne and the neighbouring town of Frechen. The grey salt-glazed stoneware, tinted by the use of slips rich in iron to achieve varying shades of brown, first became popular in the fifteenth century. By about 1600 production in Cologne seems to have come to an abrupt halt when all the potters had moved to Frechen. It was at these two centres that the majority of the bearded flasks or *Bellarmines* were produced (Pl. 3B). These jugs were obviously produced very cheaply and consequently rarely bear more decoration than a simple medallion, although a few examples covered with Gothic oak-leaf foliage are known. Later *Bellarmines* with shields of the arms of Cologne, Amsterdam, England, etc., all appear to have been made at Frechen from the late sixteenth century onwards. Production continued in this area until the eighteenth century.

Another important centre of Rhenish stoneware was situated at Raeren near Aix-la-Chapelle, although production here seems only to date from between 1565 to 1600. The majority of the stonewares follow Cologne styles, although the work of one potter, Jan Emens, active 1566–94, was particularly fine. His wares were more finely decorated than those of Cologne and included almost every technique known at the time; applied moulding, carving and pierced decoration. Some of his finest wares were decorated with reliefs copied from contemporary engravings by Adrien Collaert.

The Westerwald was the second great German stoneware centre, although wares of artistic merit are not recorded until late in the sixteenth century. The jug with the initials of Queen Anne (1702–14), illustrated in Pl. 3B, is typical of the great numbers of similar wares produced since the late seventeenth century when, in addition to insignificant small applied decorations including rosettes, lion-masks and angel's heads, greater use began to be made of incised and combed lines which acted as barriers to contain the cobalt-blue and manganese-purple colours. Production of these wares has continued to the present-day and many examples are to be seen with an impressed mark representing a stoneware jug.

The most colourful German stonewares were created at Kreussen near Bayreuth in Bavaria, in the usual brownish-grey stoneware coloured to a dark chocolate-brown. The example illustrated (Pl. 3B) is dated 1681, but specimens dated as early as 1622 are known. The fine enamel colours often used as decoration could possibly be by artists whose work is more frequently seen on contemporary German glass. A unique type of earthenware produced at Kreussen features four- or six-sided canisters with metal screw-stoppers (*Schraubflasche*).

Nuremberg

Apart from the early *Hafner*-wares made at Nuremberg there was undoubtedly a considerable production of tin-glazed earthenwares, but it is only on very slim evidence that a few dishes bearing dates in the second quarter of the sixteenth century are attributed to such potters as Hirschvogel, Nickel and Reinhard. Such pieces were nearly all discovered in South Germany and are painted only in high-temperature blue with an occasional touch of yellow, in a manner similar to Venetian maiolica. The factory established at Nuremberg in 1712 by Marx and Hemmon continued in production under various partnerships until about 1840. The mark "NB" in monogram, which was adopted about the middle of the eighteenth century is by no means uncommon and is often seen together with the signatures or initials of painters. During the first half of the eighteenth century the factory produced many fine dishes, both plain and reeded, also jugs with long and narrow necks and the common cylindrical tankard. Such wares were nearly all decorated only in blue with Baroque style scrolls, foliage or strapwork, and surrounding reserves filled with such subjects as landscapes, heraldic shields, and Biblical or mythological figure subjects.

Hamburg

The early faience factory of Hamburg appear to have made its finest wares during the middle decades of the seventeenth century; dated wares are known from about 1624 until 1657. The pieces which seem to have survived best are the large pear-shaped jugs with long narrow necks, usually decorated with a bold coat-of-arms in blue. The dishes often have similar shields or devices surrounded with panels in imitation of Chinese porcelain of the Wan Li period (1573–1619).

Hanau

Probably the most prolific centre of German faience was established at Hanau, near Frankfurt-on-Main in 1661, continuing until 1806. Unlike porcelain factories, the owners very rarely adopted factory-marks that can be easily accepted and one has to rely more often on the marks of "repairers" or throwers, or the painters' initials in order to make an attribution. The early faience of Hanau has much in common with Delftware, in that all the popular Chinese forms were copied, such as gourd-vases, and many lobed or reeded dishes. The Hanau jugs often show the distinctive plaited-rope handle, but all lack the brilliant glaze of the Dutch wares, which was achieved with their second clear lead-glaze (*Kwaart*). Blue is once again almost the only colour used when imitating the typical Chinese styles of the late Ming period. During the late seventeenth and early eighteenth centuries wares were decorated with such European subjects as landscapes and Biblical scenes which called for the complete palette of high-temperature colours. Towards the middle of the eighteenth century these typical faience styles of decoration gave way to the more popular fashion for naturalistic flowers in enamel colours.

Frankfurt-am-Main

The factory at Frankfurt-am-Main was in production from 1666 until about 1772, but once more the lack of a regular factory-mark makes certain attribution a little difficult. Their early copies of "Chinese-Delft" are very similar indeed to the Dutch wares, especially as the practice of covering the tin-glaze with a further translucent glaze was also employed (Pl. 4A). The Frankfurt copies of Chinese blue-and-white often included manganese-purple when dishes were painted with alternating panels of flowers and Chinese figures. When one of the early proprietors died in 1693 an inventory was drawn up of the stock at the time, and it is from this list that certain shapes and decorations can be identified with the factory. "Finely painted in purple" probably refers to those pieces made in a similar form to those of Hanau and painted with biblical subjects. There is little doubt that most of the finer decorations seen on wares attributed to Frankfurt are the work of such *Hausmaler* as Johann Heel.

Bayreu: -B·X   ℛ

Riß
1714   B·P·F

Bayreuth

Little is known of the early years of the faience factory
established at Bayreuth about 1713. In 1724 the concern was
taken over by the Crown-Prince Georg Wilhelm, Margrave of
Brandenburg-Kulmbach, who erected new buildings and
appointed Johann Nicolaus Grüner as manager. The early
wares were much in the style of both Hanau and Frankfurt,
but from about 1728, when Johann Georg Knöller took over
the factory for a second time, some very fine wares were
produced in the typical Baroque fashion of the day, coupling
the popular leaf-and-strapwork borders with well-painted
armorial bearings. Some of the finest pieces of Bayreuth
faience are those decorated by such individual painters as
G. F. Grebner, Adam Friedrich von Löwenfinck and J. P.
Dannhöfer; most of their work dates in the second quarter of
the eighteenth century and apart from the iron-red and black
painting of Dannhofer, their styles are very difficult to
separate from such *Hausmaler* as J. C. Jucht and J. F. Metzsch
who are known to have decorated Bayreuth faience. During
the middle decades of the eighteenth century the work of such
painters as J. G. Fliegel and J. A. Popp can often be identified
by their signatures or initials.

Ansbach

When Mathias Bauer started up the faience factory at Ansbach
in Bavaria in 1710, the Margrave, Friedrich Wilhelm of

Brandenburg, was so determined it should succeed that he prohibited the sale of Hanau and Frankfurt wares in the territory. The early wares were certainly like those produced at these two factories, but this was probably due to the fact that the painter and "arcanist", Johann Caspar Ripp, who helped to establish the Ansbach concern, had previously worked at both Hanau and Frankfurt. Once again it is the initials or signatures of painters such as Ripp, J. G. S. Popp, and Georg Oswald, often coupled with the date and abbreviated forms of "Ansbach", which enable one to identify key pieces showing the early use of a very strong blue on a blue-tinted ground, again often outlined in manganese-purple. The most distinctive wares of Ansbach were made from about 1730–60 when the painter J. G. Eberlein is attributed with pieces which were first painted in blue and then decorated further with lacquer, red and gold in order to imitate the Arita porcelains of Japan. Similar wares were made in imitation of the *"famille verte"* style of Chinese K'ang-Hsi porcelain (1662–1722).

Höchst
The factory of Höchst, near Mayence in Germany, is better known for its porcelain production from 1746 until about 1758. Adam Friedrich von Löwenfinck was probably responsible for most of the fine painting in enamel colours seen on the earliest pieces which covered almost the entire range of table-wares. Later painters, whose initials are seen together with the "wheel-mark" of the Höchst factory (as on porcelain), were G. F. Hess, I. Hess, Adam Ludwig, Johannes Zeschinger and J. P. Dannhöfer. There is a good deal of similarity in the wares of Höchst and those of Strasbourg, especially apparent in the small Rococo tureens which were painted in a comparable palette and also the large tureens modelled in the form of various birds, boar's heads, etc.

Fulda

Many of the painters mentioned as having worked at Höchst were also connected with the faience factory at Fulda, which was active from about 1741 until 1758. The body of the tin-glazed earthenware made at Fulda is dark red, as compared with the usual biscuit colour, but this was well disguised with an excellent white enamel glaze. Many Fulda wares were decorated to imitate Chinese "*famille verte*"; as at Ansbach, using the full palette of low-fired enamel colours together with gilding. The finest of such work together with copies of Meissen-type harbour-scenes are sometimes found to bear the initials "F.v.L." for Adam Friedrich von Löwenfinck.

Cassel

The Landgrave of Hesse-Cassel established a faience factory at Cassel as early as 1680, which remained in existence until about 1862, although for approximately the last ninety years the production consisted almost entirely of wares made in imitation of Wedgwood creamwares, jasperwares and other Staffordshire type bodies made in Josiah Wedgwood's days. The faience made from about 1680 until 1788 was nearly all painted in high-temperature blue in imitation of Dutch Delftware and can sometimes be identified with the letters "HL" for "Hessen-Land".

Schrezheim

Schrezheim, near Ellwangen in Württemberg, can at least boast a mark, for in 1752 after J. P. Bux had founded his faience factory, a mark was adopted that looks like an arrowhead, but it is taken to be a play upon the owner's name and really depicts a sprig of box. Apart from a large documentary altar-piece, their wares consisted of Strasbourg-type tureens modelled after nature and all the common and cheaply produced objects such as mugs, jugs and coffee-pots. These were first painted in the limited range of high-temperature colours, but in the later years were treated as if porcelain. Today's collector is more likely to come across the nineteenth-century Schrezheim earthenware made from the earlier Rococo-style moulds, finished in either a plain yellow or brown glaze.

Thuringia

Many attractive wares, such as the tankard illustrated on Pl. 4A, were made in the various eighteenth-century factories of Thuringia: Dorotheenthal, Abtsbessingen, Erfurt and Bernberg are among the best known, and nearly all have one feature in common, unusually bright, high-temperature colours. The mark "AB" monogram for "Augustenburg"; the name of a palace of Augusta Dorothea, who was the founder of the factory, is sometimes seen on Dorotheenthal faience. The wares made at Abtsbessingen from about 1740 until the early years of the nineteenth century were sometimes marked with a "hayfork" from the Schwarzburg arms.

Erfurt

The faience concern established at Erfurt in 1717 often used a similar six-spoked "wheel-mark"—as was also used at Höchst —but as the latter factory decorated only in low-fired enamel colours and Erfurt always painted in the high-temperature colours, there should be no confusing the two.

Proskau

Some interesting tin-glazed wares were made at Proskau in Silesia from 1763 until 1850, although, as was usually the case with factories that continued into the nineteenth century, the last sixty years or so were spent in the production of Wedg-wood-type wares. The founder, Count Leopold von Proskau, was only associated with the factory until 1769, when he was killed in a duel, but it was in this short period that many wares were made in the popular Strasbourg fashion together with vases filled with fully modelled flowers, decorated in excep-tionally vivid yellows, crimsons and greens.

Holitsch

There is a marked resemblance between the wares of Proskau and those made in the Hungarian factory of Holitsch. This factory was started up in 1743 by Francis of Lorraine, consort of the Empress Maria Theresa, and continued under the State until 1827. In addition to popular Strasbourg styles, some amusing tureens were produced in the form of birds, but in most cases the painting was in a typically Hungarian "peasant-pottery" style. When the factory started to produce English-style earthenwares in 1786 the standard of both pottery and decoration was very high, probably due to the fact that workers from the Vienna porcelain factory were employed. The early faience wares were often marked with "HF" monogram for *"Holitscher Fabrik"*, while the later cream-wares carry the full name "HOLICS" or "HOLITSCH".

Heimberg

The bulbous jug illustrated on Pl. 6B is of a type seen most frequently and although such pieces were made at Heimberg in Switzerland from the eighteenth century the majority seen today have been produced during the past hundred years. Almost identical wares have been made in modern times at Thoune. Of other Swiss earthenwares and faience the production from about 1600 until around 1750 consisted almost entirely of large stoves made by the *Hafner* potter, and apart from such pieces as those in the Victoria and Albert Museum, they are rarely to be seen outside the Continent.

French Pottery

Before discussing faience, the main production of the French pottery, it is well to note two outstanding and rare types of lead-glazed pottery which have both been reproduced in large numbers.

The earliest of these wares is commonly known by two different names; St. Porchaire, or more often, Henri Deux. These pieces, of which there are only about sixty-four extant examples, were made between 1525 and 1560 from a very fine white paste, not unlike the eighteenth-century English cream-ware body, but fired at a far lower temperature, and consequently much softer. The decoration was formed by inlaying dark contrasting coloured clays, the designs first having been impressed by metal stamps similar to those used by book-binders; the whole ware was then covered with a pale honey-coloured lead-glaze. Nearly all these pieces are, of course, in such national collections as the Victoria and Albert Museum and the Louvre, but there are some very good nineteenth-century reproductions in circulation (Pl. 6A), of which many were made by the Staffordshire firm of Minton in the third quarter of the nineteenth century. The finest of the Minton pieces were made by Charles Toft under the guidance of Léon Arnoux, and are usually impressed with the name of the firm.

The second type of early French earthenware worthy of note include those made by Bernard Palissy and his followers. According to tradition, Palissy (born *c.* 1510) first decided to becomes a potter after seeing examples of Henry II ware and he worked mostly at Saintes. Palissy wares are almost entirely of a decorative nature, taking a variety of forms: dishes, ewers and even large grottoes such as those ordered by Catherine de Médicis for the Tuileries in 1566. The body of these wares was a low-fired white clay which was decorated with glazes coloured with high-temperature oxides; no tin appears to have been used and where white was required the potter applied only a clear glaze to the body. Many of the finer wares were made from moulds which in turn had been taken from metal originals. They show a skilful choice and use of coloured glazes, sometimes applied to restricted areas as in the later work of Ralph Wood, and sometimes deliberately allowed to blend together in the so-called "Whieldon tortoiseshell" manner. Many of these metal prototypes are too late to have been used by Palissy himself. Probably the best-known Palissy wares are the many round or oval dishes covered with marine creatures such as fish, lizards, crabs, snails, etc., modelled in relief.

In the field of pottery there is probably no ware that has been forged so often as that of Palissy. Thus for an original piece one looks for a light body with crisp modelling covered with clear bright glazes. The many reproductions tend to be heavier, the modelling very worn as it would have been cast from a mould taken from an original glazed piece; the colours could often be well described as muddy. For example, some time ago a pair of dishes which would in any case be rather rare, were found to be just a little smaller than original pieces, and without doubt had been made from a cast taken from an original, and the result was further shrinkage when the copy was fired.

The best known nineteenth-century reproductions of Palissy wares were made by Charles Avisseau working at Tours between 1842 and about 1889, Georges Pull of Paris, and Mafra & Son of Caldas da Rainha, Portugal (Pl. 6A). The latter are probably the poorest quality and usually include a form of vegetation which would appear to have been produced by forcing clay through a mincing-type machine.

We have seen the use of tin-glazed earthenware in Spain and Italy, a technique which was soon introduced by potters from these countries into Southern France. The earliest wares took the form of crude pottery vessels and tiles which are difficult to attribute with any certainty. It was at centres such as Lyons, Rouen and Nîmes during the sixteenth century that tin-glazed earthenwares were produced which can be linked with particular areas with reasonable certainty.

Masseot Abaquesne worked at Rouen from 1530 and apart from very finely painted flooring tiles, his main production, he made many drug-jars; one order alone for a Rouen apothecary numbered 5,000 pieces. These jars were sometimes signed by Masseot or his son Laurens, and although the shapes are the same as the Italian vessels, the colours are decidedly paler and the painting rather rough.

Wares for apothecaries also appear to have been the main products of a Huguenot potter named Sigalon who worked at Nîmes during the second half of the sixteenth century. Sigalon's painting closely imitated the Italian palette and manner.

At Lyons a more pictorial type of Italian painting was attempted. The style followed that of contemporary Urbino and great use was made of woodcuts illustrating Biblical and mythological subjects. The drawing was in the rather fussy High Renaissance manner with an irritating habit of "pouring" over the edge of the dish with little attempt to contain the picture on the surface of the ware. Such pieces often have the

title of the scene depicted written on the reverse in French,
serving to make the attribution more definite.

decorax
Anevers   D.F   *3:Custodeff*
             1636

The term faience, used to describe tin-glazed pottery, does
not appear to have been employed in France until the early
seventeenth century when such centres as Lyons and Nevers
started to leave their wares in the white tin-glaze stage with
very little further decoration, a fashion which had been
popular at Faenza, in Italy, since about 1570. These wares
were probably made to more closely suggest porcelain, still
very much admired; the secret of which still remained in the
Far East at that time. Many shapes were made in this finish,
occasionally slightly decorated with heraldic coat-of-arms;
silver-shaped chargers, bottles, puzzle-jugs and vases were
made at Le Croisic near Nantes. Production of pieces decorated in this simple manner continued well into the nineteenth century.

Nevers remained the fashionable centre for faience throughout the seventeenth century, and in addition to the Baroque
taste of the Court at the time we find they also started to
produce wares inspired by Chinese blue-and-white porcelain.
While the Dutch were carefully imitating original Chinese
porcelain in Delftware, the French potters, with typical
artistic flair, were more original in that they employed
Chinese shapes but upon these they painted designs in the
European style, or blue-and-white decoration in the Ming
style on ewers following European shapes.

A similar original attitude to faience considered to have
originated at Nevers concerns the complete staining of the
tin-glaze with a dark-blue, termed "*bleu persan*" due to a
mistaken association with Persian wares (Pl. 2A). Such pieces

are generally of bold, vigorous shapes and in some cases were probably intended for garden use. The painting is either in white, or in white, orange and lemon, with the decoration consisting of flowers in the oriental style or Ming-type landscapes with Chinese figures.

The most familiar wares of Rouen are perhaps those made by Edmé Poterat (1647–96). These include large chargers decorated in blue, the painting of which is often so skilfully executed that an unwary collector would dismiss it as a transfer-print. Pendant decorations are suspended from the border of the chargers or hang down the walls of an ice-pail in a style which is termed *"lambrequins"*, a trefoil form with spirals derived from Chinese blue-and-white of the K'ang Hsi period (1662–1722). A somewhat similar form of decoration is the *style rayonnant*, where two motives alternate around the borders or edges of table wares, one spiral and leaf form being in blue on white, the other white on blue (Pl. 2A). Many may find these designs tedious or monotonous, but the technical skill of the painters cannot be denied. These designs were often further enriched with swags or garlands of fruit similar to those on Delftware or the scrollwork of *"ferronerie"* (ironwork). Often extremely monumental, many pieces were in addition decorated in the centre with the coat-of-arms of the owner in blue, apparently to suggest porcelain. Only rarely is the additional colour of a sticky orange-red, typical of Rouen, to be found together with only blue.

Since early in the eighteenth century Rouen has also made full use of the entire range of high-temperature colours as well as making a special feature of large commemorative cider-jugs which give accurate dating to current styles. By the middle of the century the Baroque style had given way to Rococo fashions, but the decorators at Rouen never really captured the true feeling of this later, insistently asymmetrical, style unless they were making direct copies of German designs.

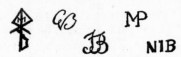

Wares made in and around Rouen were generally far below the quality of other such famous centres as Strasbourg or Marseilles, as they were heavily potted and the green-tinted and much-pitted glaze could in no way be mistaken for porcelain. Such wares have, however, remained popular with tourists and the familiar cornucopia pattern in the strong high-temperature colours of Rouen can be seen on plates decorating the walls of cafés all over France today.

It should be noted that the large (7ft. 4in. high) busts on stands of Apollo and the Seasons made by Nicholas Fouquay during the second quarter of the eighteenth century have frequently been reproduced; the original Seasons are now in the Louvre, the Apollo in the Victoria and Albert Museum.

Wares made at Rouen and Sinceny, near Laon, can easily be confused, especially if the "S" mark of Sinceny has been left off, as is the case with some of the later wares, for from 1737 Pierre Pellevé and other Rouen workmen were engaged at Sinceny in making wares in nearly all the well-known Rouen patterns.

The new collector of English tin-glazed earthenware should also note the activities of the Fauquez family at Saint-Amand-les-Eaux, 1718–92. Among their better known pieces are many painted in opaque-white on blue-tinted glaze (*bianco-sopra-bianco*), which at first glance could be confused with similar wares made at Bristol.

The faience factories of the south employed styles with free

Above (Pl. 3A), figure of a boy with a kid, tin-glazed earthenware, painted in enamel colours. French (Niderviller), 1770–1784. Ht: 7⅞ in.; figure of a boar, tin-glazed earthenware, painted in enamel colours. French (Strasburg, P. Hannong), *c.* 1755. Ht: 3¼ in.; figure of a boy sweep, unglazed earthenware. Mark, 'Terre de Lorraine' impressed. French (probably Lunéville modelled by P. L. Cyfflé), *c.* 1770. Ht: 6⅞ in. *Below* (Pl. 3B), jug, salt-glazed stoneware with blue decoration. German (Höhr-Grenzhausen), early 18th century. Ht: 6⅞ in.; jug, salt-glazed stoneware with enamel decoration. German (Kreussen), dated 1681. Ht: 8½ in.; bottle, salt-glazed stoneware with applied decoration. German (Frechen), 17th century. Ht: 10½ in.

Above (Pl. 4A), dish, tin-glazed earthenware painted in blue. Mark, 'IH' in blue. German, 17th century. Diam: 12 in.; tankard, tin-glazed earthenware painted in colours. German (Thuringian), mount dated 1760. Ht: 8½ in. *Below* (Pl. 4B), four tiles, tin-glazed earthenware in blue (Delftware). Dutch, *c.* 1760. Single tile 5 in. x 5 in.; vase and cover, tin-glazed earthenware in blue. Mark, a claw in blue. Dutch (Delft, Claw factory), *c.* 1770. Ht: 14½ in.

bold painting of an entirely different character to those of the north. Pierre Clérissy started a factory at Moustiers in the sparsely populated area north-east of Marseilles in 1679. The factory remained under the direction of Clérissy's descendants until 1783, when it was sold to Joseph Fouque in whose family the concern remained until finally closed in 1852. The early wares of Moustiers include some extremely beautiful blue-and-white dishes decorated with hunting-scenes after engravings by Antonio Tempesta (d. 1630). In about 1710 the fashion for pictorial subjects gave way to a style popularized by the "Designer to the King in the Department of Occasional Expenses", Jean Berain (d. 1711). Many of the designs, painted in a soft high-temperature blue, could well have formed a background scenery for one of the extravagant entertainments at the court of Versailles.

A further Moustiers factory was set up by Joseph Laugier and Joseph Olerys in 1739; their mark, "LO" in monogram form is frequently seen on nineteenth-century reproductions (Pl. 6A). Laugier, previously mentioned as having also worked at Alcora in Spain, first continued to decorate in the Berain style, but now using high-temperature colours of green, yellow and purple in addition to the blue as used by Clérissy (Pl. 2A). Judging from dated examples, in about 1745 Laugier and Olerys abandoned Berain styles for the more Italianate fashion of framed mythological or Biblical scene set in a border of floral swags (Pl. 2A), as well as a further new fashion comprising slightly grotesque human and animal forms scattered over the surface of the ware. A few minor concerns such as those of Jean-Baptiste Ferrat and Fouque and Pelloquin, only started to decorate in the full range of low-fired enamel colours after 1770.

The many factories of Marseilles started decorating faience in the enamel colours of the *petit feu* (low fired) about 1750, introducing a delightful style of flower painting which was so

3

accomplished and yet seemingly careless. The earliest wares attributed to Marseilles were made at Saint Jean du Désert, a nearby village, from about 1677. Like many of the painters, the founder, Joseph Clérissy, came from Moustiers and, as was to be expected, they decorated the wares in similar styles to those made at Moustiers. The rather heavy-handed painting, especially in the border patterns, is an aid to recognition of the Marseilles pieces. This factory finally closed in 1748.

A further important Marseilles factory was that of Joseph Fauchier and his son (also Joseph Fauchier), it existed from 1710 until 1789. Their earliest wares were painted in the Berain style as used at Moustiers. More particularly noteworthy were their large figures, fountains, wall-cisterns, holy-water stoups and plaques, which were painted in one or other of the two available palettes; high or low-temperature colours. It is probable that the Fauchiers introduced the pleasing method of staining the entire tin-glaze ground with a mustard-yellow. The known marks of this factory are simple F's, or the name "FAUCHIER" in full.

Probably the most copied mark on spurious French faience is the monogram "VP" (in full "Veuve Perrin", widow Perrin). The widow of Pierre Perrin was a remarkable woman in her time, since following her husband's death in 1748, she continued to raise her family and ran a successful business until her own death in 1793. The wares made at Marseilles by Veuve Perrin and her contemporaries were very similar in style and high standard achieved. They were mainly wares decorated in enamel-colours, with flowers, (Pl. 2B) fish, fruit, vegetables, insects, *chinoiserie*, etc., all applied with a complete freedom from any formality, which was a characteristic of the area in which they were produced.

During the short period of partnership between Honoré Savy and Veuve Perrin (*c.* 1753–70), the former is reputed to have introduced a fine translucent green enamel which he combined with black outlining to create some very beautiful flower painting. Savy started his own factory in about 1770, and consequently this style of painting was carried out at both factories. The *fleur-de-lis* mark which Savy adopted in about 1777 is another mark which often appears on forgeries of Marseilles faience.

Other Marseilles factories which should be mentioned include that of Joseph Gaspard Robert (*c.* 1750–*c.* 1800), who marked his wares with various forms of "R" and "JR" in monogram. Robert often used a green monochrome style of decoration similar to Savy's but usually added gilt borders which give his finer wares a porcellanous look. Antoine Bonnefoy, until about 1770 apprenticed to Robert, set up his own factory which had the unusual distinction of surviving the French Revolution and continuing in production until 1815. "B's" and "AB" monograms are sometimes accepted as the marks of Bonnefoy, but on very slender evidence. His manner of painting fish, flowers and *chinoiseries* tended to follow the popular Marseilles style, but were in a more restrained style and favoured classical shapes. The wares made at Marseilles by Jacques Borelly (or Boselli) have much in common with those he made after about 1780, when he transferred his business to Savona in Italy. His styles generally followed those of Strasbourg but in a far bolder and vulgar manner.

A peculiar French customs law made it advantageous to the French potters at Strasbourg and places adjacent to the border to sell their wares across the German frontier, with the consequence that they tended to cater for German taste and their love of Rococo, a style which had quickly been adopted after its introduction into France about 1730.

There must be few collectors of pottery who are not acquainted with the name Hannong. The Strasbourg factory, established in 1721 by Charles-François Hannong (*d.* 1739), produced those early tin-glazed wares which were generally only painted in blue following Rouen style and taking the form of large lobed octagonal dishes. These bear no factory-mark, but many examples have been identified by comparison with sherds found on the factory site. In 1732 management of the Strasbourg factory was taken over by the son, Paul-Antoine, while his brother Balthasar was given another branch of the business at Haguenau; this branch may well have made wares which were later decorated at Strasbourg.

Early pieces made under the directorship of Paul-Antoine were painted in the full range of the high-temperature colours (*grand-feu*). The painting was highly stylized and followed the fashion made popular on early Meissen porcelain of "Indian" flowers; these flowers had, in fact, been originally copied from Chinese and Japanese porcelain.

In about 1750 Hannong recruited several German painters and chemists conversant with the manufacture of hard-paste porcelain and the painting of such wares in the more colourful pallette offered by the *petit-feu*, or low-fired enamel colours.

With such new colours Hannong commenced painting his Rococo-shaped wares with the more naturalistic style of flower-painting also practised at Meissen, the *Deutsche Blumen*; this style soon became known as "Strasbourg flowers" and was in turn copied by many other French factories. The palette of Strasbourg included a rich purple-red (Pl. 2B), which was used to emphasize the Rococo-moulded edges of such large wares as tureens, the smaller plates usually having a simple narrow line of purple or brown. Apart from practical wares, Paul-Antoine Hannong produced many figures, dishes and tureens modelled after nature (Pl. 3A). Many of the German-style figures were undoubtedly modelled by Wilhelm Lanz, who remained at Strasbourg until his return to Frankenthal in 1754.

In 1753, the well-known arcanist Joseph-Jacob Ringler arrived in Strasbourg from Höchst. With the aid of Ringler's knowledge concerning the manufacture of hard-paste porcelain, first gained in Vienna, Hannong himself started to manufacture the same material, but the opposition of the French soft-paste porcelain factory of Vincennes was such that he was forced to transfer his manufacture to the German city of Frankenthal.

Following the death of Paul-Antoine Hannong in 1760 the Strasbourg faience factory was directed by his son Joseph, until 1780. Both types of flower painting were continued, the highly-stylized and the naturalistic, but now often outlined in black in a heavy manner.

Strasbourg faience was so popular that the styles were often copied in the eighteenth century, particularly at Niderviller, where the ground colour is decidedly creamier than the brilliant white of Strasbourg. Lunéville, another contemporary copyist, replaced the rich purple-red with a dull crimson. Many of the more recent forgeries are prone to crazing (crackling of glaze), though the marks "PH" in monogram for Paul Hannong (1739–60) and "IH" for Joseph Hannong (1762–80) are among the most commonly faked marks recorded.

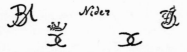

The factory at Niderviller, near Sarrebourg in Lorraine, was established in about 1754 by Baron Jean-Louis Beyerlé. Having encouraged many of Hannong's most important workers to transfer their skills to his manufactory, he too was forced to sell out in 1770 by the powerful monopolies enjoyed by Sèvres, to Count Adam Philibert de Custine, General of the Royal Armies, a man who was obviously in great favour at Court, for he eventually made both faience and porcelain; until he "lost his head" in 1793, despite siding with the revolutionaries. The wares of both Beyerlé and Custine were more in keeping with the quieter French feeling for Rococo than the wilder German taste, and in many cases are obviously modelled from ideas "borrowed" from Chantilly or Vincennes-Sèvres porcelain. The flower-painting was more delicately handled in keeping with the finer material of porcelain. For a later style of decoration, the entire ground of a dish or vase was painted to imitate wood (*décor bois*), often with a crimson monochrome painting as if on canvas or paper seemingly pinned to the wood. Apparently popular at the time, it is a style which is not appreciated by collectors today.

Almost without doubt, the factory of Niderviller produced more faience figures than any other factory. The bases, composed of grassy mounds or Rococo scrolls, are reminiscent of those modelled by Johann-Wilhelm Lanz at both Strasbourg and Frankenthal. The preference at Niderviller was certainly for the country-peasant type (Pl. 3A) rather than gallants or courtiers; these were generally tastefully decorated with delicate representations of fine patterned fabrics. The mark of Beyerlé is "BN" in monogram in manganese-brown, black or blue, while the luckless Count used two interlaced "C's" under a crown in similar colours.

Probably among the most common but nevertheless genuine, pieces of French faience constantly on the market are the birds and *chinoiseries* boldly painted in the crimson and green palette of such minor Eastern French factories as Lunéville, Saint-Clément and Les Islettes. Among the earliest wares of the Lunéville factory (established 1723) are the well-known recumbent lions which were probably intended for garden decorations. These large animals were obviously extremely popular as the nineteenth-century concern of Keller and Guérin continued to produce them. The simple plate illustrated on Pl. 2B is typical of the early nineteenth-century wares produced at both Lunéville and Saint-Clément. The latter also made a type of faience which is also easily identified as the decoration simply consisted of gilding on Neo-classical forms.

The French faience factory of Sceaux, situated on the outskirts of Paris, produced wares which probably came nearer to approximating the look of fine soft-paste porcelain than any other undertaking in France, which was achieved despite the harsh monopolies enjoyed by the factories of Vincennes and Sèvres. Although the factory at Sceaux was established as early as 1735, it was not until 1750 that the proprietor, De Bey, aided by Jacques Chapelle, began to produce fine wares decorated with enamel colours following the Rococo styles of the Sèvres factory as far as the cheaper material would permit.

From 1775 Sceaux enjoyed the patronage of the Admiral, the Duc de Penthièvre, accounting for one of the many marks employed in which the letters "SP" (Sceaux-Penthièvre) are inscribed over an anchor, "CS" (Chapelle-Sceaux) 1759–c. 1763, "GS" (Glot-Sceaux) 1772–93 were also used, as well as a *fleur-de-lis* which could easily be confused with the mark of Savy of Marseilles.

Lunéville is better known for the soft earthenware (*terre de pipe*) figures and groups which were left "in the biscuit" (Pl. 3A). The majority of these were modelled by Paul-Louis Cyfflé and date from about 1755. The little *Sweep* which is illustrated is typical of this modeller's work and is one which became popular in Staffordshire, where the same figure can be found in the coloured glazes associated with the Ralph Wood family in about 1775. In 1766 Cyfflé established his own hard-paste porcelain factory in Lunéville where he made similar biscuit figures until 1780; many of his moulds were acquired by the Niderviller factory at this date.

The introduction into France of Wedgwood's popular cream-coloured earthenware made it necessary for many of the faience factories to turn to making similar wares; Pont-aux-Choux (Paris), Chantilly, Niderviller, Creil and Montereau all produced varying standards of creamware. The Paris concern of Pont-aux-Choux was established in 1740, but it was not until 1765 that they commenced the production of creamware which they advertised as *Manufacture Royale des terres de France a l'imitation de celles d'Angleterre*. The body was of fine quality and easily distinguishable from English wares by the preference for high relief flower decoration and silver shapes (Pl. 5A).

The earthenwares made at Chantilly since the late eighteenth century are more of a clear-glazed white earthenware and lack the pleasing yellowish glaze. The hunting-horn mark, which also appears on Chantilly porcelain, occurs on these wares too, sometimes with an added "P" for Pigory, a contemporary Mayor of Chantilly.

In 1781 two Englishmen, Charles and James Leigh started a *faïence fine*, or creamware, factory at Douai, a venture which continued until 1820. These popular productions mainly consisted of the fretted openwork style associated with Leeds. Apart from the mark of "Leigh & Cie" or "Douai", the names of "Martin Dammann" and "Halfort", who ran similar short-lived factories at Douai in about 1800, are to be seen.

Of all the creamwares made in France since the late eighteenth century, the productions of Creil and Montereau are most frequently encountered. The Creil factory, established in about 1794 was amalgamated with Montereau in the early nineteenth century and production continued until 1895.

Most Creil wares are decorated with transfer-prints in black enamel, but those depicting fables, landscapes, portraits and well-known buildings were most probably added at Sèvres in the decorating-shop of Stone, Coquerel and Legros d'Anisy (Pl. 5A). Later proprietors included Leboeuf and Milliet (L. M. & Cie) 1841–85 and Barbuet et Cie (1885–95).

The town of Apt (Vaucluse) has been an important French pottery centre from the early eighteenth century until today. Their finest wares have a buff body with a thick yellow glaze prone to crazing. A love of Rococo clearly distinguishes these from Staffordshire ware, although a form of agate and marbling could well be copied from English wares. The only recorded mark is a "VA" monogram for Veuve Arnoux the widow of Antoine Arnoux who continued the factory until 1802. Similar wares were produced at nearby factories by Bonnet until the mid-nineteenth century, and the descendants of César Moulin until 1852.

Belgium

The earliest tin-glazed wares manufactured in the Netherlands were the work of Italian immigrants or their pupils, with the result that the forms and decorations of wares attributed to such centres as Antwerp, etc. follow Italian fashions and are best referred to as Netherlandish—rather than the later ill-used term "Delft" (these early wares will be discussed under the chapter on Dutch pottery).

Not until the early eighteenth century did the tin-glazed wares made at Brussels start to show signs of originality. Such pieces were made by Phillippe Mombaers, who in 1724 took over the direction of the factory which his father had started some twenty years earlier. The main output was apparently concerned with large tablewares in such naturalistic forms as various birds, fishes and vegetables. Although no regular factory-mark appears to have been used, these wares can often be identified by the peculiar "running" habit of the glaze which resulted in the colours being streaked with the white tin.

Faience had been made at Liége from the middle of the eighteenth century. The first venture, which was established by Baron von Bülow, was apparently unsuccessful for after a succession of directors and owners, the factory was purchased by Joseph Boussemaert under whose direction it flourished. Even the best work attributed to Liége was lacking in originality and consisted mainly of wares decorated in imitation of Rouen or Strasbourg. The factory continued until 1811.

A later faience factory was established at Andenne in 1783 by Joseph Wouters. He is said to have broken with his partners and to have established a factory of his own in 1794 which continued under the direction of B. Lammens until 1820; the painted initials "BL" are consequently attributed to this factory, together with "BD LS & CE" impressed, sometimes in a cartouche with the words "Grande Manufacture Andenne". In addition to faience he also produced white and cream-coloured earthenwares decorated with either blue painting or transfer-printing.

From the late sixteenth century there were many towns in southern Belgium and adjacent parts of eastern France where salt-glazed stoneware vessels were produced. Most of these vessels were in the same style as those made in the Rhineland but were at first of a slightly lower fired material with a duller finish. All the popular shapes of "bearded" bottles (*Bellarmines*), barrels, jugs and pilgrim-flasks were produced with the common rust-colour glaze. Later wares were made in the grey and cobalt-blue colours of the German Westerwald type.

Holland

The earliest pottery of the area known today as Holland was, of course, made before 1609 when Holland, together with six other provinces of the northern Netherlands, first became independent of the County of Flanders and duchy of Burgundy.

At times it is difficult to separate the tin-glazed wares made in Antwerp from about 1510 and similar Italian wares, as such pieces were generally the work of Italian potters like Guido di Savino (or Andries) of Castel Durante who was known to have been making maiolica in Antwerp in the first half of the sixteenth century. Therefore it is more correct to refer to the early tin-glazed wares of such cities as Antwerp, Haarlem, Rotterdam, Amsterdam, Middelburg, and other centres in Friesland as maiolica, and reserve the more popular term Delftware for the vessels and tiles made in the city of Delft and elsewhere in Holland from the mid-seventeenth century onwards.

Probably the earliest documentary examples of Italian-type maiolica made in the Netherlands are the tiles preserved in the Abbey of St. Bavon, Ghent, painted in the popular green and manganese palette of the earliest Italian wares. An early example of the work attributed to Guido Andries is the tile-paving at The Vyne in Hampshire, laid at the time of the re-building in 1520.

A particular group of maiolica made in Antwerp since the middle of the sixteenth century illustrated the popularity of designs based on ironwork (*ferronerie*), strapwork, and scrolls, designs which first appeared in engravings dating from about 1540. Another style of painting suggesting Italian origin is to be seen on wares made in the North Netherlands from about 1570–1600; here we find artists who were undoubtedly acquainted with contemporary wares of Faenza and Venice, decorated with such fruit as pomegranates and grapes, but painted in a brighter palatte. On dishes made in the mid-sixteenth century in Antwerp we first see the so-called "blue-dash" around the edges which is so familiar on seventeenth-century English wares.

Tin-glazed earthenware vessels became as popular with the apothecaries in the Netherlands as they had in Italy, Spain and the Near-east, with the result that the familiar drug-jars and spouted drug-pots, often only painted in high-temperature blue, can safely be attributed to such northern centres as Haarlem, Middelburg and Amsterdam. A type of Nether-landish ware that is often encountered can easily be confused with the "grotesque-arabesque" style found first on Italian maiolica made at Urbino (see p. 42), but is probably as much as fifty years later than the prototypes; the potting is usually thinner and the orange tones less bright.

As a result of the trading by the Dutch East India Company (founded 1609) with both China and Japan, the Netherlandish potters soon became familiar with Far Eastern porcelain and from this time the overdecorated maiolica styles gave way to earthenwares made in imitation of the finer oriental porcelains; wares which we normally associate with the many potters who from about 1620 were to work in the town of Delft; hence the term "Delftware", which we can now rightly associate with Holland.

Delft was also a centre of the beer-brewing industry, but toward the middle of the seventeenth century many breweries fell out of use and their premises were taken over by potters. The result of this was that many factories retained the name of the brewery, i.e.: "The Golden Flowerpot", "The Porcelain Bottle", "The Hatchet" and "The Two Little Ships".

Normally the craftsmen associated with making and decorating pottery were not eligible for membership of craft Guilds, but the Guild of St. Luke in Delft (founded 1611) made an exception in the case of those concerned with the fine earthenware reproductions of oriental porcelains and permitted one or two master-potters to become members each year. The partial destruction of Delft in 1654, caused by an explosion, helped to provide further premises for the flourishing pottery trade in the swift rebuilding programme which immediately followed.

The finest Delftwares were made between 1650–1710 after which time the Far Eastern hard-paste porcelain was shipped to Europe in very large quantities and in addition similar true porcelain was available from the Meissen factory of Augustus II near Dresden in Saxony.

The potters of Delft and such other towns as Rotterdam, Amsterdam, Gouda and Dordrecht where similar wares were made, suffered a further crisis in about 1760 when English salt-glazed stoneware and cream-coloured earthenwares were imported in large quantities and much preferred to their softer tin-glazed wares. In 1764 the Dutch potters regularized the use of authorized factory-marks and only from this date can marks be accepted as trustworthy, for there is good evidence that prior to this date many factories fraudulently added the marks of more popular and successful rivals; this is particularly the case with the "AK" mark of Adrianus Kocks and "APK" of Adriaen Pijnacker.

The first aim of the Delft potters was undoubtedly to make their wares look as similar as possible to the original Chinese blue-and-white porcelain. With this idea in mind they refined their clay bodies to a far greater extent than had been the case with the earlier Italian wares. In addition they often went to the trouble of adding a clear glaze, known as *kwaart*, upon the opaque tin-glaze, which sometimes makes it difficult to be certain of the composition of the body without actually handling the object. During the last quarter of the seventeenth century the Dutch potters reproduced almost every type of blue-and-white Chinese porcelain associated with the reign of the Emperor K'ang Hsi (1662–1722). The mark most frequently seen on wares of this period is "AK" in monogram form. While this mark is in some instances attributed to Albrecht Keiser of "The Two Little Ships" factory, it is more likely to be that of Adrianus Kocks of "The Greek A" factory. His bills dated 1695, for the superb tall hyacinth and tulip-vases to be seen at Hampton Court, are still in existence. These vases were decorated according to the designs of Daniel Marot; similar sets can be seen at Chatsworth (Derby-shire) and Dyrham Park (Gloucestershire). Despite the popularity of these "pagoda-like" vases, there do not appear to be any documentary records actually showing them in use. Each tier is an independent dish with the "nozzles" for the flowers protruding from each angle of the usually octagonal form. When these are filled with water and used as flower-vases the result is far from pleasing, and it would therefore seem more reasonable to assume the bulbs were planted in fibre and positioned to allow growth through the hole. Perhaps a reader will be able to produce some firm evidence in the way of a Dutch flower-painting of the period.

The Dutch pottery painters were especially fond of out-lining their painting, a process called *trek*. Decoration outlined in manganese-purple is often found in pieces bearing the mark of Samuel van Eenhorn also of "The Greek A" factory.

From about 1650 onwards the Delft potters also created European forms which they decorated in the style of contemporary Dutch oil-painting, but only on rare occasions can such landscapes or figures be attributed with certainty to any particular decorator.

A much-sought-after form is the model of violins, the

originals of which date from about 1710–20 and are decorated with interesting figure-subjects. But as is usual with such rare pieces, there are many more fastidious reproductions made in more recent times.

Dishes painted with such subjects as interiors, fishing-scenes, landscapes symbolic of the months and Biblical events generally come from about the middle of the eighteenth century and often bear the axe-mark of "The Hatchet" factory which continued until 1802, or the flower-mark of "The Rose", which continued under various owners until 1854. Other late marks frequently seen are a claw, "The Porcelain Claw", (1662–1850), and "The Three Bells", looking like three little trees (1671–1850). A flattened form of baluster-shaped vase (Pl. 4B) with a lid surmounted by a crude version of a Chinese Dog of Fo became popular in the mid-eighteenth century, but when painted with small scenes depicting typical souvenir-type windmills, etc., these are best avoided by collectors as they almost certainly date around the late nineteenth century. Similar popular forms whose numbers indicate present-day manufacture are the various little donkeys, etc., bearing an "AG" monogram. Until some sure knowledge of this common mark can be learnt, one must not rule out northern France as a possible attribution.

At the beginning of the eighteenth century the Delft potters extended their high-temperature palette to include green, iron-red and yellow which enabled them to copy the *famille verte* colours of the K'ang Hsi period and the Japanese porcelains of Arita. The most impressive pieces made in this polychrome style include the large sets of five vases made to garnish high mantle-pieces, chests or cabinets, usually comprising three covered jars and two vases. These suites continued in popularity for many years and were made in Worcester soapstone porcelain and the late Bristol hard-paste.

Two types of black-ground wares were made at Delft. The

earlier wares were completely covered in black, with green, yellow and blue decoration most probably inspired by Chinese *famille noire*. Later, black was painted around reserve panels containing oriental decoration.

The same range of high-temperature colours was employed by many of the early eighteenth-century Delft potters for the decoration of plates and dishes painted with elaborate baskets or pots of flowers. Similar decoration of a very high standard also occurs on panels of small tiles painted to form a complete picture.

From the middle of the eighteenth century greater use was made of the full range of colours offered to the decorator who used low-temperature enamels fired in a muffle-kiln. These colours were particularly preferred for the imitation of the red, blues and gilding of the so-called Japanese brocaded wares of Arita. As the Dutch potters became more conversant with European porcelain fashioned in the popular Rococo styles, they too started to apply Meissen-like harbour-scenes and "Watteau" figure-subjects in typical Rococo shapes, often combined with such liberal use of gilding that the term *Delft dorée* was introduced to describe this novel treatment of a long-established technique which was now entering into a decline.

The practical potters of Holland had very little success with figures or wares other than true potter's shapes. Probably among the most difficult wares to correctly date are the countless jugs in the form of cows and model shoes, both of which were manufactured for nearly a hundred years. One particular type of dish which has frequently been mistaken for English work depicts the Stadtholders William III, IV or V with their families. These were usually made at such centres as Rotterdam or Friesland rather than at Delft itself.

There were many seventeenth-century centres other than Delft renowned for their excellent tiles, which were usually made for wall decoration rather than floor-paving. The early tiles are of a reddish clay and at least twice the thickness of the later quarter-inch thick tile of a biscuit coloured clay, which is often seen in England as fireplace surrounds.

In the late seventeenth century the early use of the maiolica-type palette gave way to designs in either blue or manganese-purple. The decorative subject matter included cavaliers, horsemen, soldiers, ships, *putti*, grotesque sea-monsters, mythological figures, Biblical scenes and simple landscapes (Pl. 4B). It is only possible to date many such tiles by the quality of the painting which declined as the eighteenth century continued. Some of the more exciting designs, the soldiers on prancing horses for example, have become popular enough to justify present-day manufacture.

Before leaving the subject of Delftware decoration, it should be noted that in Delft there were also a number of independent enamellers whose work is to be seen on a large variety of wares and materials other than Delftware. The hand of these independent workers is apparent on Chinese, Japanese and Meissen porcelain, English delftware and Staffordshire salt-glaze stoneware and cream-coloured earthenwares. The easiest to identify are probably the salt-glazed wares painted in the customary palette of pink, green and a brick-red.

During the last quarter of the seventeenth century the Dutch potters made some very fine red stoneware teapots in imitation of those exported from China together with the tea; the original oriental unglazed red stonewares were made at Yi-hsing. The Spanish or Portuguese term *boccaro* ware is a faulty term best forgotten. Several Delft potters appear to have been able to make this fine red ware, the best known being Lambertus Cleffius and Lambertus van Eenhorn of "The Metal Pot Factory", Samuel van Eenhorn and Arij de Milde. The mark of the latter, a running fox with "ARY. DE. MILDE" appears most frequently on these important wares which are certainly an early link between Chinese originals and the refined red wares of John and David Elers who worked both in Fulham and Staffordshire, to eventually the finest red stoneware ever produced, that of Böttger of the Meissen factory.

Scandinavian Earthenware

Copenhagen

The first Danish factory to produce tin-glazed earthenware was apparently that of the Store Kongensgade factory in Copenhagen. Johann Wolff, who is believed to have been a pottery painter from Nuremberg, took charge of the factory from its beginning in 1722 but was succeeded two years later by Peter Wartberg.

The most prolific period of the concern was between 1727 and 1749, when Johann Ernst Pfau was director; during this period their productions chiefly followed styles of Holland and Nuremberg. The early wares tended to continue the more formal Baroque styles, but when in about 1750 the popular demand was for pieces in Rococo style the blue painting was usually carried out in a pleasing careless fashion. It is only the occasional marked specimens that help to separate these Danish wares from the mass of similar pieces being made elsewhere on the Continent. While the marks attributed to Wolff and Wartberg are very rarely seen, the "IP" monogram of Johan Pfau is by no means so uncommon. The factory closed about 1770.

Kastrup

Both the other principal Danish factories were established

later in the eighteenth century. The factory at Kastrup, on the island of Amager near Copenhagen, was set up in 1755 by the Court-Architect Jacob Fortling with the aid of workmen from the Strasbourg factory of J. A. Hannong; in consequence the styles of Kastrup tend to follow the lighter Rococo fashions of France rather than German faience. Such wares as were made under Fortling's supervision are sometimes identified by an "F" in manganese-purple, but such a single letter is always subject to some doubt. During the latter part of the eighteenth century some typical English style creamwares were made by Christian-Westerholdt Mantzius who impressed his wares "CW" over "M" in an oval.

Østerbro

The third major faience factory of Denmark at Østerbro was very short-lived, because six years after Peter Hoffnagel had commenced his manufacture, the proprietor of the Store Kongensgade objected on the grounds that he alone had been granted the privilege to make faience and Hoffnagel was forced to close down. Wares that were produced during this period appear from the factory records to have nearly all been in the usual Rococo styles, but sometimes gilding was used in addition to the more customary blue and purple high-temperature colours. The rare documentary pieces ascribed to Hoffnagel were marked either "Ø(ster)B(ro)F(abrik)" and the initials, or the full name of "J. Hasrisz" a little-known painter.

Schleswig

At the time when the Saxon arcanist Johann Christoph Ludwig von Lücke established his faience factory, Schleswig was a Danish province. In 1756, one year after his arrival, Lücke departed and the factory had about eight successive owners before closing down in 1814.

The initials seen on the best of the Schleswig wares indicate that the finest productions were made during the period from 1756–73, when first the two brothers Otte, and later Johann Rambusch, were proprietors. During this period the majority of the pieces were painted in manganese-purple enabling them to evade the order which banned the importation of blue-and-white wares from Copenhagen. Apart from the interesting bowls in the form of a bishop's mitre (intended for a local punch known as "bishop"), many unusually large pieces were produced such as tureens, baskets, trays and even table-tops, nearly all of which were decorated with purple flowers on Rococo forms. Among the many more common wares produced were plates decorated with the ever-popular onion-pattern of Meissen, but now in purple rather than blue. The full name of Schleswig is a known, but rare, mark, more usually the letter "S" is seen together with the initials of one of the various proprietors and those of little known painters.

Kiel

Some of the best decorated wares made in Schleswig-Holstein in the eighteenth century were produced at Kiel in a factory owned by the Duke of Holstein. There is little doubt that the very fine wares decorated in the full palette of low-fired enamels were made during the time that production was under the supervision of J. S. F. Tännich from Strasbourg (1763–c. 1769) and his successor Johann Buchwald of Eckernforde (c. 1769–c. 1772).

The painting on the best of Kiel pieces is so superior to that of most other contemporary factories that they must have been either very expensive or sold at a loss, this is especially the case with many of the fine *pot-pourri* vases (*Lavendelkrukke*) which have not only very good relief decoration of fruit, flowers and foliage on the pierced lids, but equally well-painted landscapes or figure-subjects on the sides of the vessels.

Other popular shapes included plates, flower-pots and wall-fountains, all showing a good use of moulded and pierced decoration which was often emphasized with crimson edging. The pieces have much in common with the wares of Strasbourg, where in fact many of the Kiel painters came from.

The marks of Kiel follow very much the normal practice of several Scandinavian factories, i.e. Kiel or "K", together with the initials of the current proprietor and the painter. The factory came to a close in 1788.

Rörstrand

Johann Wolff had already proved during his short stay at the Store Kongensgade factory in Copenhagen that his knowledge of faience production was scanty. In 1725 Wolff's application to establish a factory in Sweden received the blessing of the Board of Commerce and after a small beginning in the city of Stockholm itself, a newly formed Swedish Porcelain factory was built at Stora Rörstrand, outside the city; and within two years production had advanced sufficiently to justify a visit from the King. The early productions of Rörstrand were far from original and tended to follow the popular style of Dutch, German and French wares. For the first fifteen years or so all pieces were decorated in only blue but during the 1740's the full range of the remaining high-temperature colours were used to advantage.

Following Wolff's dismissal in about 1728, other various foreign managers were hired until 1740, when a Swede, Anders Fahlström was appointed. From this time until about 1767 the factory enjoyed a period of prosperity which resulted in the production of many fine wares. In 1758 the full palette of enamel colours and gilding was used on wares which by now had acquired a distinctive Swedish style that had probably been introduced to the factory by such well-known designers as Christian Precht and J. E. Rehn.

It is difficult to say whether the painting of white-glaze on a tinted ground, *"bianco-sopra-bianco"*, was suggested by English or French wares (the lace-like style adopted would suggest the latter), whereas the later practice of using transfer-prints was almost certainly inspired by English potters, who had been decorating wares in this manner since about the middle of the century. In view of their fragility it is amazing how many of the large table-trays, such as were also made at Schleswig, have survived.

As early as 1771 this Swedish factory was finding it necessary to also manufacture cream-coloured earthenware in order to compete with the exported wares of Josiah Wedgwood and other English potters and from the time of the retirement of the manager Jakob Örn in 1796, the factory produced hardly anything except English-type earthenwares (Pl. 5B).

Today, in addition to many fine commercially produced earthenwares and porcelains, this factory is well-known for its encouragement to modern potters and designers such as Carl-Harry Stålhane, Hertha Bengtson, Sylvia Leuchovius and Marianne Westmann, some of whose work will undoubtedly number among the antiques of the future.

Marieberg

Johann Ludwig Eberhard Ehrenreich came from Germany to Sweden in 1747 as the Court dentist to King Frederick I, and after the death of his patient in 1751 he became determined to set up a pottery and porcelain factory, which he eventually did at Marieberg, on Kungsholmen, Stockholm, in 1759. The factory almost immediately produced wares superior to those of the rival Rörstrand factory, but financially, affairs became so difficult that in 1766 Ehrenreich's backers had no option but to dismiss him.

Many of the fine wares made in the first six years of the Marieberg factory were left entirely in the white, relying upon form, glaze and applied decoration for effect. Apart from high-temperature blue, a fine range of enamel colours were introduced which included a rich green, a Strasbourg-like crimson, purple and black, all of which surpassed the enamels of Rörstrand. All these fine colours were used to decorate tureens, covered jars and a type of vase peculiar to Marieberg known as a "terrace-vase" in which the base consists of gracefully whirling Rococo scrolls or similarly winding staircases.

In 1766 Pierre Berthevin, who had previously worked at the French soft-paste porcelain factory of Mennecy, succeeded Ehrenreich as manager. From this date the adoption of French styles, both on figures and useful wares, was very noticeable. About this time Marieberg started to decorate its wares with transfer-prints. This technique proved very popular and was continued on a much larger scale by Henrik Sten who succeeded Berthevin in 1769. In 1782 the factory was sold to Rörstrand and from that time until it finally closed in 1788, the main output was of cream-coloured earthenwares.

When marked, the faience of Marieberg has a similar three-crown device to that seen on the soft-paste porcelain of the same factory, but in some cases it also bears the actual date of manufacture, such as 13/1/69, indicating 13th January, 1769.

Stralsund

From 1720–1814 Stralsund in Pomerania belonged to Sweden, it was here that Johann Buchwald established his faience factory in about 1755. Very few wares of any distinction were produced until after 1766 when Ehrenreich, who had previously founded the Marieberg factory, took over. Predictably the wares produced under the guidance of the new lessee were in many ways similar to those of Marieberg; with vases and tureens all being heavily decorated with rather impractical, but pleasing, high relief decoration consisting of flowers, leaves, birds, masks and figures. In 1770 the factory was partially destroyed by an explosion and although restarted by Johann Giese in 1772, very few pieces worthy of note were again produced before the concern closed in 1792.

The rather complicated marks used during the Ehrenreich period almost suggest an algebraic equation, with an arrow-like device, accompanied with such detail as the initials of both the proprietor and painter, and the date.

Herrebøe

The most important faience factory of Norway was founded at Herrebøe, near Friedrichshald, in 1757 by Peter Hoffnagel. Virtually the only colours used on their Rococo-style forms were cobalt-blue and manganese-purple. The decoration seems to have been hastily sketched-in, scrollwork, shells, flowers, figures in landscapes, all show this same feeling of spontaneity so appropriate to the fashion of Rococo.

There seems to have been no regular form of factory-mark, "HB" for "Herre Bøe" over painters' initials is sometimes seen and on one rare example the word "HERREBOE FABRIQUE" is written in full, but it is considered that many wares were left unmarked.

Part III

Porcelain

Medici and other Italian porcelains

It would be beyond the scope of this book to spend too long on the subject of Medici porcelain since it is extremely rare: there are only fifty-nine recorded examples. However, we are told that there could still exist about fourteen unrecognized examples of this first ever European porcelain.

Credit for the introduction of soft-paste porcelain into Europe in about 1575 is given to the Grand Duke Francesco I de'Medici. The concern seems to have been entirely devoted to the production of wares for the personal needs of the family rather than having been a commercial undertaking; thus production was limited. Records show that the wares were almost certainly fired at the factory of the contemporary maiolica potter Flaminio Fontana who, in 1578, was paid for firing twenty-five to thirty pieces of porcelain. After the death of the Duke in 1587 no other serious European attempts to produce porcelain appear to have succeeded until one reaches the last quarter of the seventeenth century when soft-paste porcelain was produced at Saint-Cloud in France.

Briefly, the Medici porcelains consist of about 80% white clay together with 20% of the ingredients of glass (frit). The original recipe, preserved in Florence, includes white clay from Vicenza (probably kaolin), while the ingredients of the frit are shown as white sand, rock-crystal, calcined lead and tin. The porcelain was first fired to the biscuit state, decorated in underglaze-blue, sometimes with a manganese-purple outline, and then covered with a transparent lead-glaze which called for a second firing. Most of the surviving wares are faulted in some way. The glass-like, white body was prone to distortion, the glaze is obviously too thick and often underfired, showing minute bubbles and sometimes large crackles. Only one example, painted with the other high-temperature colours of green and yellow, is known.

Although the Italians were probably familiar with Chinese porcelain as early as 1295, when Marco Polo returned to Venice; there is no slavish imitation of the oriental wares to be seen in these early examples of soft-paste porcelain. The shapes are simple, traditional twin oil and vinegar bottles, jugs with trefoil-shaped pouring lips and tall, square-section bottles, usually associated with spirits; plates sometimes have a central boss, as if to seat a ewer. Other wares show the influence of contemporary maiolica and bronzes.

The underglaze-blue painting of Medici porcelain was probably subject to more Oriental influence than the forms themselves and far outnumber any pieces with such European styles as grotesques, cameos and coats-of-arms. The former painting styles can usually be correlated with the styles popular on the Chinese wares of the Chia Ching (1522–66) and Wan Li (1573–1619) reigns.

Of the fifty-nine known examples all but a few have as a mark, a drawing of the dome of Sta. Maria de Fiore, the Cathedral of Florence, in underglaze-blue; this form of mark was undoubtedly suggested by Chinese reign-marks. Some pieces have the six-ball device of the Medici arms as a mark, while others remain unmarked.

Venice: Vezzi factory

Venezia.

The first hard-paste porcelain factory to be established in Italy was that of Francesco Vezzi (*b.* 1651–*d.* 1740). Vezzi was a wealthy goldsmith who, having made his fortune, apparently sought fame by being the first person to produce hard-paste porcelain in Italy. The Meissen factory of Saxony had been in production since 1710 and Du Paquier had been making similar wares in Vienna from 1719. Although Hunger had found it necessary to enlist the aid of the Meissen kiln-master Samuel Stölzel when assisting Du Paquier, by 1720 he had apparently learnt sufficient to be able help Vezzi to produce true porcelain. Vezzi's factory continued to flourish until 1727, when the faithless Hunger returned to Meissen. Here he revealed Vezzi's reliance upon clays from Saxony with the result that export of the clay was instantly prohibited and the concern was forced to close down. It has furthermore been suggested that the factory would have failed in any case because of mismanagement by Vezzi's son, Giovanni, in whom the father had entrusted control of the concern.

The rare porcelain of Vezzi was often undoubtedly influenced by early Meissen and Vienna, but many original and interesting styles were also introduced. The porcelain leaves little doubt as to the source of the material, for the usually fine white body compares well with Meissen. Occasionally a slight grey or cream tinge is noticeable but the glaze is usually clear and bright with only a slight brown tinge apparent where application was too generous.

Of the many shapes produced, teapots appear to have been a favourite. Globular in form, thickly thrown, they often show the spiral "wreathing" marks more commonly associated with the hard-paste porcelain of Bristol. Even more characteristic of Vezzi are the familiar, octagonal teapots with acanthus leaves in moulded, high relief decoration. These teapots often bear some of the best painting to be seen on Vezzi porcelain, the subjects of homely-looking characters in fancy dress painted in a bright enamel palette in which strong iron-red predominates. Many wares were copied direct from the Chinese *blanc-de-Chine* made at Tê-hua in the Fukien province, applied prunus designs sometimes being picked out with enamel colours.

Decoration in underglaze-blue was attempted at Venice as early as at Meissen but, in most cases has resulted in the blackish-grey blues, so often the result of a too high temperature. These blue designs, which are often of *chinoiserie*, are sometimes carefully outlined in a bronze-coloured gold.

The majority of Vezzi porcelains are marked with various forms of the word Venice: "VENEZIA", "Ven^a" or "Va", in either gold, underglaze-blue or red enamel. Arthur Lane, in *Italian Porcelain* (Faber) points out several instances of the mark being fraudulently added to later wares—even to earthenware. These, he suggests, are usually so badly painted, in style often dating far later than 1727, that identification is usually made easy.

Venice: Cozzi factory

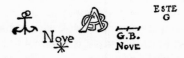

After the failure of Vezzi's porcelain manufacture in 1727, little porcelain was made in Venice until the establishment of the Cozzi factory in 1764. The only noteworthy production during this long interval was that started in 1758 by N. F. Helwelcke, a porcelain retailer. The few pieces of porcelain which can be attributed to this short-lived concern are of a hard-paste porcelain with a slight yellow appearance. The glaze is thin and has a waxen look. Tea bowls and saucers, jugs and teapots are nearly all decorated in a palette including a thick brownish-red which is used for border patterns and picking out relief detail. These wares are invariably marked with the letter "V" (for Venice), either incised, in relief or in red enamel. The factory ceased in 1763.

Soon after he had started his hard-paste porcelain factory in Venice in 1764, Geminiano Cozzi was granted many privileges from the state. Subsidies for the manufacture of maiolica were granted in 1769 and again in 1781 to help make creamwares to compete with the English wares. The factory managed to survive invasions and occupations by foreign troops until it finally closed in 1812. Within a year of commencement Cozzi had produced enough wares of a sufficiently high quality to warrant orders for state gifts. Cozzi's porcelain never equalled that of Meissen. Like the wares of most other Italian factories the body was grey and had a somewhat ill-fitting, wet-looking glaze. The shapes were usually more thickly potted than other European porcelains and the colours can best be described as harsh. In comparison, however, the gilding was excellent (Pl. 7A).

The Italian porcelain modellers never really understood the Rococo styles, for their approach was too fussy. Their treatment of tall coffee-pots is typical: ill-formed handles overlaid with leaf forms together with the insertion of the pouring lip into the wall of the vessel are all highly characteristic of the factory, but nevertheless, not displeasing. Similarly, the painting of the table-wares also falls far below the standard of most German hard-paste factories. By about 1780 the influence of Sèvres was apparent in the introduction of wares with dark blue borders broken with marbling and with sparsely applied gilding around red-painted panels containing scenes after Veronese, Tintoretto and Tiepolo.

When enamel colours are used on Cozzi figures they generally include an addition to the typical Italian porcelain palette of brownish-reds, purples and blues and an unsatisfactory yellowish-green. The flesh tones are usually not stippled in the popular Italian fashion. Very few figures bear the red-anchor mark of the Cozzi factory with the result that a certain amount of doubt exists over the attribution of figures, especially those left white. Arthur Lane suggests that particular features of Cozzi figures, as opposed to those of Le Nove, are the general weakness both in expressions and composition, the loosely-arranged Rococo scrollwork and the later rockwork bases supporting the groups in pyramidical form, as listed among the factory's wares of 1783. Circular pedestals with Neo-classical swags and masks in relief are also a typical feature of this period.

Apart from a few genuine replacements, the porcelain of Cozzi does not appear to have warranted the attention of the deliberate fakers.

Le Nove

Pasquale Antonibon was already a successful maiolica manufacturer when he started experimenting with the material of porcelain at Le Nove, near Bassano, in 1752. Although assisted by German and French workers, success was not achieved until 1762. He submitted examples of his wares to the Venetian Board of Trade and was immediately granted all the usual privileges but, because of ill health, he was unable to make full use of the benefits granted to him and in 1773 retired. The maiolica factory was continued by G. M. Baccin who, towards the end of the century, made some very good creamwares following English styles. The porcelain manufactory was eventually (1781) taken over by Francesco Parolin; he was succeeded, in 1802, by Giovanni Baroni who continued as director until the factory closed in 1825.

Many of Antonibon's workers were engaged by Cozzi and, consequently, the similarity in the early wares of both factories is extremely confusing; both have the same greyish paste with a glaze that, when thick, has a brownish hue and the same enamel palette. After Parolin took charge in 1781 there was a decided improvement in the material, colours and gilding of the Le Nove wares.

The Italian porcelain factories do not appear to have conformed to the popular European tastes as is so marked elsewhere. Baroque styles continued well into the 1760's, while misunderstood Rococo and neo-classical styles flourished together and continued into the early years of the nineteenth century.

Among the most pleasing wares produced at Le Nove are the fan-shaped *jardinières*. First introduced at Vincennes, these flower vases were apparently made first by Antonibon in maiolica and continued into the next century.

One of the most prolific decorators of Le Nove porcelain was Giovanni Marconi, who was with Parolin for most of his long stay at Le Nove. Marconi's signature appears in full on several examples, showing his preference for Herold-type harbour scenes as depicted on Meissen, and rural romances.

From the time of Baroni's directorship many of the wares show the increasing vogue for Empire styles but his main concern appears to have been with the manufacture of creamcoloured earthenware with painted decoration of mythological scenes, as first produced by the artist Le Brun in the seventeenth century.

According to contemporary documents, Le Nove was

producing porcelain figures as early as 1765 but these are mostly difficult to attribute with any degree of certainty. Domenico Bosello, who was with Parolin, is credited with the modelling of the typical, robust, Italian peasants, grouped on rocky bases, often with the word "NOVE" incised beneath. These rock-like bases were often pierced with holes into which flowers or grass was inserted.

Le Nove wares often have the signature of the painter, or the date, etc., painted or scratched into the enamel in rather obscure places and careful searching can sometimes be rewarding. The usual factory mark, adopted in 1762, was a six-pointed star, made up of three crossed strokes, more like an asterisk. The word "Nove" often appears either incised or in gilt.

Este

The wares produced at Este are so rarely seen by collectors that I shall touch only briefly upon the histories of the three factories that existed there. The first of these concerns was started by Jean-Pierre Varion in partnership with Gerolamo Franchini, a goldsmith, but they appear to have parted before any porcelain was produced. Varion died in 1780 but his widow took a workman from Le Nove into partnership and in 1781 they were granted rights to produce porcelain. Franchini continued alone after the departure of Varion, but there is no evidence of his having produced any porcelain. The few examples of porcelain figures with the incised mark of "Este" are all of a hard, creamy-coloured porcelain, usually standing on separate bases, and are now considered to have been modelled by Varion.

There were several other minor factories producing hard-paste porcelain in the late eighteenth century. Andrea and Guiseppe Fontebasso produced wares at Treviso until about 1840 which included simple covered bowls and cups with such initials as "G.A.F.F." (Guiseppe Andrea Fratelli Fontebasso), or the name of the painter Gaetano Negrisole. Similar wares are said to have been produced at Vicenza (1793–1800) and Angarano (1777–1780) but they have not been distinguished from the wares of Le Nove, etc.

Turin

As early as 1743, G. G. Rossetti had succeeded in producing a greyish hard-paste porcelain at Turin; he was assisted by Helchis, the painter from Vienna. Apart from a few rare examples preserved in the Turin Museum, little is known of this obviously short-lived venture.

Vische

As the same museum possesses only three marked examples of the porcelain made at Vische in about 1765, it is fairly obvious that the company formed by the Conte Francesco Lodovico Bicago de Vische could have had little success. The mark of a "W" and trefoil sometimes attributed to this factory is much more likely to be that of a minor German factory.

Vinovo

In 1776 G. V. Brodel, assisted by P. A. Hannong, from Strasbourg, established a hard-paste porcelain manufactory at Vinovo, near Turin. Brodel retired in 1778 and, as the result of Hannong's mismanagement, the factory was sold in 1780. The factory then flourished under the directorship of Dr. Gioanetti until 1796 when the country was invaded by the French. Gioanetti started up again in 1815 and work continued under G. Lomello until finally closing the factory in 1820. The creamy porcelain with a glassy-looking glaze is in appearance more like an early French soft-paste procelain but is, never the less, hard-paste.

During the formative years of the factory Hannong must have played a large part in dictating the style of the wares to be manufactured, for the forms and decorations seen in French faience from Strasbourg are in evidence throughout the first period of production at Vinovo. Characteristic are the many tall teapots, jugs with long necks, Rococo handles, scroll feet and vegetables serving as knops on tureen covers. Even the faience-style painting includes the strong crimson enamel which is such a characteristic of the Strasbourg palette.

Similarly, Vinovo figures show a marked resemblance to the models of Lanz at Frankenthal and those of Cyfflé at Lunéville. More original, however, was the work of the modeller Carlo Tamietti; his many models, made between about 1776 to 1796, are nearly all in the Neo-classical style and include Roman emperors, gods and goddesses, as well as medallion portraits of the Savoy family. These figures are usually left undecorated. The marks of Vinovo are $\overset{+}{v}$, in underglaze-blue or incised, sometimes together with "DG" (Dottore Gioanetti), or "L" (Lomello).

Doccia

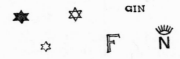

Through the generosity of the Marchese Leonardo Ginori-Lisci, the late Arthur Lane, in *Italian Porcelain*, was able to shed a great deal of new light upon the early years of the important porcelain factory of Doccia. The founder of the factory was Carlo Ginori who, in 1735 started to manufacture a hard-paste porcelain at Doccia, near Florence. He gathered around him a competent staff, including such people as J. C. W. Anreiter von Zirnfeld, chief painter, his son Anton, painter, and Gaspare Bruschi and his son Giuseppe, modellers. According to mid-eighteenth-century writers, the output from Doccia was prolific but there was some doubt as to whether the factory would survive, a forecast which has, of course, failed to materialize as the factory flourishes today.

The early hard grey porcelain was certainly a poorer material than that used by the majority of German factories and between about 1770 to 1790 this body was often completely hidden by an opaque tin-glaze but, from the late eighteenth century, a fine and typical white hard-paste was produced.

The pieces made by Carlo Ginori between about 1740 to 1757 by no means rank with the best porcelains of the period but their distinctive appearance usually offers very little difficulty to even the new collector in the matter of identification. The Baroque-style tea and coffee-pots are heavily potted with spouts in the form of snakes and high-domed lids, the cups are tall and without handles while the majority of the plates are deep enough to be used for soup and usually have a wavy edge like that of French faience. Many of the early pieces were painted in underglaze-blue, the distinct grey tone and the "salt-glaze" appearance of the glaze suggesting that the wares were fired at a rather excessive temperature. Another distinguishing feature is the application of the underglaze-blue designs by a stencil. Use was also made of the Chinese fashion for *blanc-de-Chine* vessels with double walls, the outer wall being pierced to emphasize the naturalistic flower patterns. Side by side with these rather coarse wares there were produced many finer examples which are often signed, or obviously by the hands of the Anreiters, but such pieces are now rarely encountered outside national collections.

From 1757 until 1791 Doccia was directed by Lorenzo Ginori, under whose direction many new and improved shapes and materials were introduced. The early crude tea-pots were henceforth produced in a far more pleasing material and were more finely potted; practical lugs were added to lids to lock them into the necks of the vessels and so prevent accidents. The tall cups were given handles, usually of a distinctive *chinoiserie* shape which must have been highly impractical. Handles and loops for lids were made in the naturalistic crabstock style of Whieldon and Astbury pottery or in the form of fruit and vegetables. Tureens with their stands are often to be seen sprinkled with fussy, bell-like flowers more usually associated with mid-nineteenth-century German wares.

It is usually the wares covered with the opaque tin-glaze that are so easy to identify, especially when they are painted in the palette of Japanese Arita porcelain. An interesting dated bowl, cover and stand in the Victoria and Albert Museum bears the initials of Giovanni Battista Fanciullacci, whose fine paintings are sometimes based on engravings in *Les métamorphoses d'Ovide*, together with the date 1783.

In the early years of the nineteenth century the wares included kaolin, which probably came from France, resulting in some fine "egg-shell" porcelain pieces often decorated with blue and gold *chinoiserie*.

For many years a great number of the Doccia wares, decorated with figure subjects in relief, have been, wrongly, attributed to Capodimonte. As early as 1745–55 Doccia were producing some extremely finely modelled plaques copied from the work of earlier sculptors; large vases were similarly produced with full relief figures over-painted in the full enamel palette with gilding, which usually showed the distinctive flesh colouring achieved by stippling the enamel to the glaze and often giving the appearance of bleeding from the pores. Cups, teapots and plaques were treated in a similar manner on a much smaller scale, as illustrated on the late example shown on Pl. 7A. Many of these mythological subjects can be found to have their source in sixteenth-century sculptures and bronzes. There is no evidence whatsoever to suggest that any ware of this type was ever made in the soft-paste porcelain of Capodimonte.

The archives of the Doccia factory include a price list, dated about 1760, which leaves no doubt as to when cups are listed as being "with figure subjects in low relief". Similarly, the fairly common cups and saucers are described as "Saucers with garlands in relief, painted". The relief wares are not known in a tin-glaze and original pieces can probably all be placed before 1780.

There are several explanations as to why obvious Doccia ware became increasingly important when it was connected with the rarer Capodimonte. Whatever the original cause, the Doccia factory certainly seems to have catered for popular demand and, from about 1860, produced many table-wares in this fashion (Pl. 7A), even going to the extent of adding a crowned "N" which was, of course, originally the mark of the Royal Naples factory. Crowned "N" pieces were never made at Capodimonte. If the material is soft-paste, then such wares as simple table pieces could possibly be from the Royal factory at Naples. If the porcelain is a hard-paste, then it could be either nineteenth-century Doccia or, more probably, from the Thuringian factory of Ernst Bohne at Rudolstadt, established 1854, who also used the crowned "N" mark in addition to such other marks as anchors, all in underglaze-blue.

There should be no confusion between the Capodimonte soft-paste figures and those made at Doccia in a hard grey paste with unevenly applied glaze which often shows fine cracks, and the orange tinge of iron where the body is un-protected by the glaze. The early figures are mostly based on the *Commédia dell'Arte* (Italian Comedy) and are lively, pleasing little figures in typically exaggerated, theatrical poses, usually set on a simple, square base, painted to suggest marble and almost invariably decorated in the enamel palette dominated by iron-red. The Italian modellers loved the grotesque; dwarfs, pygmies, sea-monsters and sphinxes were all produced in miniature, sometimes serving as a practical sweet-meat dish by the addition of a small dish and sometimes with screw holes to support wooden pedestals, etc.

The factory lists indicate that, after about 1780, a good many figure groups were left white; such figures are usually arranged around a tree, on a hollow, rock-like base which required additional strengthening cross-struts. Briefly, the modellers of late eighteenth- early nineteenth-century Italian porcelain figures were undoubtedly greatly influenced by the nation's long history of fine sculpture and, within the limitations of their material, they certainly managed to recapture in porcelain, the early, true Baroque spirit.

The factory mark, introduced in the late eighteenth century, was a six-pointed star in blue, red or gold; it is sometimes solid and at other times is formed by two overlapping triangles (The Star of David). "GINORI", "GIN" or "GI" is often found impressed on wares made after the mid-nineteenth century.

Capodimonte

True Capodimonte porcelain, made between 1743 and 1759 at the factory established by Charles of Bourbon, is extremely rare and an amateur collector would be exceptionally fortunate to discover a piece by chance. Charles, the son of Philip V of

Spain, was keenly interested in the excavations at Herculaneum in 1738 and his interest in porcelain may well have been initiated by his marriage to the grand-daughter of Augustus II, the founder of the Meissen porcelain factory. His attachment to the Capodimonte porcelain factory was so great that, upon his succession to the Spanish throne in 1759, he arranged to transfer the entire personnel and necessary equipment to Spain, where it became known as the Buen Retiro factory. The mark used both at Capodimonte and Buen Retiro is the same Bourbon *fleur-de-lis* and there is, consequently, much confusion over the wares of the two factories.

The records shed more light on wares made before 1750 than those made later. After several unsuccessful attempts, by various "would-be" arcanists, to produce a high quality, soft-paste porcelain, Gaetano Schepers, in about 1744, produced an exceptionally fine porcelain which remained in production until the factory's removal to Spain. The chief modeller, Giuseppe Gricc, was similarly employed for the entire period between 1743–59.

The soft-paste porcelain of Capodimonte is certainly of a higher quality than that produced at Buen Retiro. It is very translucent and generally pure white. By comparison, Buen Retiro porcelain is decidedly yellow with an unusually tight-fitting glaze for soft-paste and it occasionally has a matt-like finish which Arthur Lane suggests might have been deliberately produced as it is an ideal surface for the enamel painted decoration. The Capodimonte soft-paste porcelain was apparently easier to work with than the contemporary French material and, consequently, far thinner table wares could be produced. These nearly all show the influence of German Baroque styles which is an invaluable guide to distinguishing between the early Capodimonte and the later Buen Retiro, which favoured the Rococo. The finest example of Rococo-style Capodimonte, the "Porcelain Room" in the palace of

Capodimonte, can still be seen today. This was originally erected between 1757 and 1759 in the Royal Villa at Portici and moved to its present situation in 1865.

During its first three years the factory's output primarily consisted of "toys" (i.e. snuff-boxes, cane-handles, etc.) and tea-services. Many of the early boxes were modelled by Gricc in the form of shells, often decorated with beautifully painted portraits of ladies under the inside cover. Inventories in the Neopolitan State Archives include precise descriptions of many of the smaller table-wares and such decorative scenes as battles, seascapes, landscapes, figure-subjects or cupids can, almost without exception, be attributed to the painter Giuseppe della Torre. The painting of both monochrome and polychrome flowers is attributed to Maria Caselli.

Little evidence exists to show that Buen Retiro produced many table-wares and, consequently, the majority of these pieces are attributed to the Capodimonte factory. The earlier plates and dishes are similar in form to much of the mid-eighteenth-century French faience, often having heavily mould-ed rims which were probably intended to minimize the risk of warping. It is a great shame that Capodimonte wares are so rare, for their style of painting is, perhaps, one of the easiest to identify: the enamel is usually applied by stippling which often gives the impression of "bat-printing" (introduced into Staffordshire about 1805), while the flesh tones, applied in this same "dotted" manner, are often decidedly violet in hue. Landscapes usually show violet and orange-red cloud-forms.

The beauty of Capodimonte porcelain is best revealed in the many figures modelled by Gricc, who is recognized as one of the most versatile modellers. Lovers, Italian Comedy characters and fisherfolk, together with religious subjects, feature in the great variety of models by him and all have one outstanding characteristic: very small heads. All these groups are placed on simple mounds or rock-like bases, rather than on the more elaborate, Rococo bases, giving them a much more animated appearance.

Buen Retiro

The British were responsible for the destruction of the Buen Retiro factory in 1812 together with all its records. However, some documents do survive and these show that the transfer from Capodimonte to the new factory, in the grounds of the Buen Retiro Palace, near Madrid, in 1759, involved the transportation of 88 tons of equipment, which included a certain amount of porcelain paste, and the removal and resettlement of 44 of the staff with their families. The administration of the factory by Giovanni Tommaso Bonicelli, continued until 1781 when he was succeeded by his son Domingo (d. 1797). Schepers, who had introduced the fine porcelain body, was acting director until about 1765, when he was succeeded by Gricc, the modeller.

The wares of Buen Retiro never reached the perfection of those of Capodimonte. After many preliminary difficulties they were eventually placed on the open market, just before the death of Charles III in 1788 but, being so costly, attracted few customers and the showroom was closed in 1800.

Visitors to Spain can see many fine collections of Buen Retiro porcelain in the major museums of Madrid and, in the Palace of Aranjuez (thirty miles south of the capital), it is possible to see a "Porcelain-Room" similar to the one at Portici. The Aranjuez room is larger and shows the same large Rococo mirrors, surrounded by high relief Chinese figures, in similar exquisite porcelain to that of Capodimonte, which suggests that these panels were some of the first wares made after the transfer, using Italian clays or later imported materials. This room was probably completed about 1765.

Upon arriving in Spain, Gricc appears to have adapted his modelling style to suit the popular taste for large-scale

Rococo. Conspicuous among his many models made between about 1760 and 1770 are those which include robust cherubs similar to the carvings in many Bavarian churches. The Italian clays were apparently soon expended, for the majority of figures attributed to Buen Retiro are of a clay having more the appearance of cream-coloured earthenware. The figures created in this Spanish factory still retained many earlier features, but the material was obviously less easy to manipulate. Consequently the figures tend to be large to the point of clumsiness and the colours loud and garish, sometimes suggesting the Staffordshire enamels on Enoch Wood type figures of about 1790. Rocks again appear to be the most popular form of bases, often being roughened to give the effect of moss. The earlier subject matter mostly centred around peasants, but as popular taste for the Neo-classical style increased so such mythological and classical subjects as Venus and Cupid, Prometheus and the Vulture and other compositions, inspired by sculpture, were included in the modeller's repertoire. Only occasionally are the rock-like bases replaced by more appropriate plinths, painted to imitate marble.

The two sons of Gricc the modeller are credited with producing, during the last 20 years of the factory, large vases in the Neo-classical style and biscuit porcelain plaques, vases and flowers, coloured to imitate the popular blue and white jasper-wares of Josiah Wedgwood.

Naples

The Royal Factory of Naples was established in 1771 by Ferdinand IV, son of Charles III. Naples had become an

attractive centre for all scholars of antiquities since the first
excavations at Herculaneum in 1738; the findings had been
kept secret until the official publications were produced in
1757. In 1763 the British Minister in Naples, Sir William
Hamilton, was involved in similar excavations on the site of
Pompeii. Thus the time was ripe for the establishment of a
porcelain manufactory which Ferdinand hoped would match
that of Capodimonte, set up by his father twenty-eight years
earlier. The factory was built beside the harbour and near the
Royal Palace of Naples.

Many former Capodimonte workers were re-engaged, but
very little was achieved until 1779, when Domenico Venuti
became Director. He set about hiring the services of well-
known modellers and skilled workers from other long-established factories, such as Vienna and Le Nove. Among their
first successful productions were large services, intended as
gifts to foreign heads of state, which generally included
centrepieces of biscuit porcelain figures.

The porcelain produced at Naples consisted of a very
translucent, glassy paste. The early wares tended to be rather
yellow, but during the 1780's a fine white or creamy body was
consistently produced. The early wares show a distinct
relationship in form to Capodimonte of the later Rococo
period and the same stipple-style painting of fruit, flowers and
groups of people is also present (Pl. 7A).

From the time of Venuti's appointment in 1781, the wares
of Naples took on a style far more suitable to both the material
and the period. As well as Neo-classical forms, the decoration
was directly related to the current discoveries at Herculaneum
and Naples. In the case of two large services, the "Herculaneum Service" and the "Etruscan Service", books were
published to fully identify and explain the various illustrations
which appear on the porcelain. Pieces from the "Etruscan
Service" are still in the collections at Windsor Castle.

Among the more common pieces of table-wares often seen in antique shops today, are the many plates decorated with a central medallion enclosing peasants in traditional costume, with a border design of wreaths or the Pompeian fret.

The most interesting of the late eighteenth-century figures are probably those of fashionably dressed individuals casually strolling along, either alone or in pairs. They appear off-white, either glazed or in the biscuit. This realism is further heightened by the fact that they rarely have additional bases and balance, sometimes rather precariously, on their own feet.

Naples is, of course, the factory that first employed the much-copied crowned "N" as a mark. It should be remembered that, unless the material is soft-paste porcelain, the mark is fraudulently added (as discussed under Doccia). A further Naples mark is "F.R.F." (Fabbrica Reale Ferdinandea) in blue, red or black enamel under a crown.

Meissen

There must be very few people today who are not acquainted with the term "Dresden porcelain" but, perhaps many may not realize that this is an alternative for the more correct term of Meissen. During the eighteenth century the word Dresden was sufficient to describe this first European, hard-paste porcelain factory; in fact, the Derby factory, when first established in 1756, was known as "The New Dresden" factory. Today this term causes a great deal of confusion, for in the mid-nineteenth century many small factories and porcelain decorators appeared in the city of Dresden itself, making and decorating inferior wares in the style of early Meissen and even adopting marks which are sufficiently similar to the crossed swords of the original factory to confuse collectors.

For many years much of the wealth of many European states had been used to purchase the only true porcelain available; that made in China from the time of the late T'ang dynasty (A.D. 618-906). This porcelain was exported to Europe from the seventeenth century onwards in fantastic quantities by the ships of the East India Companies, together with cargoes of tea and silks.

When Augustus II, King of Poland, succeeded to the title of Elector of Saxony in 1694, one of the first demands he made of his economic adviser, Ehrenfried Walther von Tschirnhausen, was for an organized survey of the country's mineral wealth, particularly relating to semi-precious stones and the materials necessary for the manufacture of fine glass comparable to that of Bohemia. It is possible that Tschirnhausen himself decided to try to impress Augustus by discovering, at the same time, the materials used by the Chinese in the production of their high-fired, white porcelain.

However, the man who is most generally connected with the re-discovery of true porcelain in Europe is Johann Friedrich Boettger, a young alchemist who had claimed to know the secret of turning base metals into gold. Frederick I, King of Prussia, first patronized him, but having failed, Boettger was forced to seek refuge in the neighbouring state of Saxony in 1701. Here he was immediately detained by order of Augustus II who was also anxious to make gold. By 1705, having still not justified his claims, Boettger was imprisoned as an impostor in the Albrechtsburg fortress at Meissen, 12 miles from Dresden. He was released two years later upon the condition that he should assist Tschirnhausen with his research into the composition of true porcelain. Before discovering how to make white porcelain, Boettger produced some very fine hard red stonewares, made in imitation of the Chinese red-wares produced at Yi-hsing (the term *boccaro* is faulty and best forgotten).

Although Tschirnhausen died in 1708 many authorities now consider that too much of the credit for the introduction of porcelain at Meissen goes to the young alchemist, Boettger, for unglazed porcelain appears to have been produced in small quantities before Tschirnhausen's death. In the following year Boettger claimed to have produced a white porcelain, both glazed and decorated, a claim which was apparently true, for in 1710 the establishment of the Royal Saxon Porcelain Manufacturer was officially announced.

Because of lack of financial support, very little white porcelain appears to have been made before Boettger died in 1719. Care had, however, been taken to acquire his secrets, for the manufacture of the glaze and firing techniques was known to Dr. Wilhelm Heinrich Nehmitz, and the preparation of the porcelain body to Dr. Jacob Bartelmei. The early years following the establishment of the Royal factory seem to have been mostly devoted to the production of a fine red stoneware, a material which has never been equalled. It was said, by Boettger, to possess "the hardness of porphyry . . . and is something entirely new in the world, as much on account of its brilliant polish as also for its everlasting durability". The value of this red stoneware was that, being of such fine grain and so hard, it could be polished and engraved as if it were a natural semi-precious stone. The colour, the result of the presence of oxide of iron in the clay, varied according to kiln-temperature, from the light-fired, orange-red to a high-fired, grey-black. A brilliant black glaze, made by the addition of manganese and cobalt oxides, was introduced for use on the lighter-fired and consequently porous-wares. Similar pieces were apparently made long after the death of Boettger, for

Above (Pl. 5A), bowl and cover, earthenware (agateware). French (Apt), *c.* 1770. W.: 7⅝ in.; dish, white earthenware with printed decoration. Mark 'Creil' impressed and 'Stone Coquerel et le Gros-Paris-par brevet d'Invention' in black. French (Creil, printed in Paris), *c.* 1815. W.: 9¼ in.; sugar-bowl, cream-coloured earthenware. Mark, a 'fleur-de-lis' in gold. French (Paris, Pont-aux-Choux), late 18th century. W.: 6⅛ in. *Below* (Pl. 5B), plate, creamware painted in black and brown. Mark, 'FMG' over 'N' impressed. Italian (Naples, Giustiniani factory), late 18th–early 19th century. Diam: 9¼ in.; tureen and cover, creamware. Mark, 'BG' in red. Italian (Naples, Biagio Giustiniani), *c.* 1815. L.: 9¼ in.; plate, creamware painted in colours. Mark, 'RORSTRAND G' impressed. Swedish (Rörstrand), late 18th–early 19th century. Diam: 10 in.

Above (Pl. 6A), candlestick, earthenware, imitation Henri II ware. French (M. Rondel), 1860–1870. Ht: 7 in.; plate, tin-glazed earthenware, painted in imitation of Moustiers ware. French (Paris, Samson's factory), 1889. Diam: 10¼ in.; jar and cover, earthenware decorated in imitation of Palissy ware. Portuguese (Caldas, M. Mafra's factory), *c.* 1880. Ht: 7¼ in. *Below* (Pl. 6B), teapot, tin-glazed earthenware painted in yellow and green, imitation 18th-century Faenza ware. Italian (Florence, Cantagalli's factory), *c.* 1888. Ht: 5 in.; cup, tin-glazed earthenware in lustre, imitation Deruta. Italian (Florence, Cantagalli's factory), *c.* 1888.; bottle, earthenware with enamel decoration. Swiss (Heimberg), *c.* 1878. Ht: 6 in.

Above (Pl. 7A), sugar-bowl and cover, soft-paste porcelain enamelled in colour. Mark, 'FRF' monogram under a crown in blue enamel. Italian (Naples), *c.* 1775. Ht: $4\frac{5}{8}$ in.; plate, hard-paste porcelain in enamel colours. Mark, an anchor in red. Italian (Venice, Cozzi factory), *c.* 1765. Diam: $8\frac{1}{8}$ in.; teapot, hard-paste porcelain in enamel colours. Mark, a crowned 'N' impressed. Italian, *c.* 1860–70. Ht: $4\frac{3}{4}$ in. *Below* (Pl. 7B), jug, hard-paste porcelain in enamel colours. Mark, a shield in blue. Austrian (Vienna), early 19th century. Ht: $4\frac{1}{4}$ in.; plate, hard-paste porcelain in red enamel. Meissen porcelain decorated by F. F. Mayer of Pressnitz, mid-18th century. Diam: $8\frac{3}{4}$ in.; tankard, hard-paste porcelain in black enamel. Austrian (Vienna, Du Paquier's factory), *c.* 1725. Ht: $4\frac{1}{2}$ in.

Above (Pl. 8A), tea-caddy, hard-paste porcelain painted in enamel colours. Mark, '54' in gold. German (Meissen), *c.* 1735. Ht: 4¾ in.; cup and saucer, hard-paste porcelain painted in under-glaze-blue. Mark, crossed-swords and star in blue (Marcolini period). German (Meissen), 1774–1814. Diam of saucer: 5¼ in.; chocolate-pot, hard-paste porcelain painted in enamel colours. Mark, crossed-swords in underglaze-blue. German (Meissen), *c.* 1745–50. Ht: 5⅜ in. *Below* (Pl. 8B), group of children, hard-paste porcelain painted in enamel colours. Modelled by J. J. Kaendler. Mark, crossed-swords in underglaze-blue. German (Meissen), *c.* 1750–55. Ht: 5⅞ in.; figure of a map-seller, hard-paste porcelain painted in colours. Mark, crossed-swords in underglaze-blue. German (Meissen), *c.* 1745. Ht: 6¾ in.

examples are known incised with the crossed-sword mark (the arms of Saxony), which was not adopted until about 1723.

The earliest types of Boettger stoneware were styled in the Chinese taste and, in many cases, the moulds were probably taken direct from original oriental pieces.

Later and more ambitious vessels were produced imitating the silver forms of the famous court goldsmith, J. J. Irminger, and showing such popular contemporary features as acanthus leaves, masks, lion's heads, gadrooning, beading and pierced open-work, also to be seen on contemporary silver. Figures were made in this material but are extremely rare, the majority being in National collections. The early pieces were cast direct from Chinese originals and consisted, mainly, of popular deities. The Italian Comedy figures which followed were far more original. W. B. Honey has suggested that they were possibly modelled by some of the well-known ivory carvers, active in Dresden at the time.

It should be noted that a little later two similar red stone-wares were made in Germany. The first was from a factory at Plaue an der Havel (Brandenburg), where a red stoneware was produced for the Prussian Minister, Frederick von Görne, who had purchased the recipe from one of Boettger's workmen in 1713. These pieces are easily identified by their inferiority in every respect; material, colour, pottery and form. A second factory was set up at Bayreuth during the 1730s, but this is a much softer ware with dark-brown glaze and was usually decorated with silver or gilt *chinoiseries*. A yellow earthenware with a lead-glaze was also produced.

The earliest pieces of white Meissen porcelain were made from China-clay (kaolin) and a calcareous flux, such as marble or alabaster; they had, apparently, not discovered china-stone (petuntse) at this time. In consequence these wares show a distinct yellowish hue, as compared with the bluish-grey of Chinese porcelain. This could, of course, also be due to the presence of a small amount of impurity, such as iron, in the clay.

Although, at first, the white porcelains were made in the same silver-forms as stonewares, shapes were soon produced which emphasized the plasticity of the new material; the applied prunus decoration, often seen on Chinese porcelain, being replaced by more appropriate vines or rose sprays. Practical tablewares, such as tea and coffee pots, tankards and vases, were all produced. Boettger had had little success with his enamel decoration and often resorted to the simple lacquer colours; the difficulty was to find a suitable flux which would fuse his colours to the hard glaze without burning them away at too high a temperature. The earliest documentary piece, showing the arms of the Electress Sophia of Hanover (d. 1714), is in the British Museum and shows a palette very similar to that used by the German glass enamellers. Boettger's most successful coloured decoration was his pinkish lustre, derived from gold. Among the most successful figures made in the early white porcelain are the grotesque dwarfs after the engravings of Callot which were published in Amsterdam in 1716.

In 1720 Stölzel, the Meissen workman who had assisted Du Paquier to establish the rival factory at Vienna, took the risk of returning to Meissen. He assured himself of a warm welcome by bringing with him Du Paquier's most valued painter, Johann Gregor Herold, together with his knowledge of fine enamel colours which could be successfully fused to the hard-paste porcelain, and which were to make the Meissen wares world famous.

Within a short time Herold became artistic director of the factory and, until the arrival of Kaendler, in 1731, all the table-wares and vases were made with sufficient space to advantageously display the superb painting carried out under Herold's direction. From this time until the start of the

Seven Years' War, 1756, Meissen dictated the porcelain fashions of Europe with its ornamental table-wares and figures, almost all heavily influenced by the popular taste for Baroque design.

For many years Augustus had been acquiring great quantities of Chinese and Japanese porcelain and, in 1717, he had purchased a large palace which was renamed the *Japanisches Palais*, and filled it with his porcelain collection. This was available to such people as Herold who was inspired by what he saw to produce many fine garnitures of vases; these vases came in sets of five, three covered and two beaker-shaped, and were intended to decorate high chimney pieces. Herold soon introduced many fine ground colours including a yellow, similar to that associated with Chinese wares made for the Emperor. The vases were decorated in the famous Herold *chinoiseries* and some documentary pieces are signed by the painter himself, although the factory list of workers employed in 1731 shows that many other painters were engaged in the "fine painting of Japanese figures". One must not confuse J. G. Herold with Christian Friedrich Herold, a painter who was employed at the factory from 1725–77.

Similarly, the painter, Adam Friedrich von Löwenfinck is also considered to be the inventor, if not always the actual painter, of the series of Meissen wares decorated with peculiar composite animals which have quite a "nightmarish" appearance. He is associated with more wares than he could possibly have painted in his lifetime. In the 1731 list he is noted as a painter of the Oriental or "Indian" flowers, so often seen on genuine "A.R." vases. On a genuine Meissen piece, the "A.R." monogram (for "Augustus Rex") in underglaze-blue, suggests that the vessel was made for the personal use of the King. It is often seen on wares made between 1725 and 1730 and less frequently on those made during the lifetime of Augustus III, who died in 1763. Unfortunately this mark has been used a great deal on very poor copies of Meissen porcelain, made and decorated in the second half of the nineteenth century.

In about 1730 the early *chinoiseries* started to give way to busy harbour scenes which include both Oriental and European characters. These paintings which, in many cases, are the work of C. F. Herold, were probably inspired by Augsburg engravings of Italian port scenes by Melchior Kysell after J. W. Baur (Pl. 8A).

Such paintings contained within the reserved panels on the coloured grounds, can to a certain extent be dated by the gilt framing. The early Herold *chinoiseries* are generally contained within a crowded gilt frame of complicated Baroque-like curves (*Laub und Bandelwerk*) and feathery scrolls, the gilding being lined with mauve or crimson enamelling. As one moves towards the mid-eighteenth century, these surrounds become less ornate and the panels are often framed in a simple gilt lobed surround or even left entirely unframed.

In its early years Meissen had little success with underglaze-blue painting, since their firing temperatures were even higher than those used in China and caused the underglaze-blue to fire to a greyish-blue or black. In about 1721 David Köhler, an arcanist, succeeded in producing a satisfactory blue, more in keeping with the Chinese porcelain of the K'ang-Hsi period (1662–1722). Köhler died in 1725 and it was not until early in the 1730s that a good underglaze-blue was available once more.

In about 1740 Meissen introduced what was to become their most famous flower-painting. These naturalistic European flowers were termed "*Deutsche Blumen*" and are attributed to Johann Gottfried Klinger, who employed a pale, blue-grey enamel for shadows which tended to lift the flowers from the white porcelain ground (Pl. 8A). At the same time insects, such as butterflies were also painted in the surrounding ground, often being used (as at the Chelsea factory) to hide any small blemishes or impurities in the white ground. There is reason to believe that such other painters as J. G. Heintze and G. S. Birckner also painted botanical flowers in a similar manner.

Apart from the early figures in Boettger's brown stoneware very little attention was paid to producing figures until in about 1727 Johann Gottlob Kirchner was appointed as a modeller, although a year later he was dismissed as being "frivolous and disorderly". His successor was Johann Christoph Ludwig von Lücke, who lasted only eight months because of his incompetence. In 1730 Kirchner was re-appointed and made some very fine large animals, vases and figures to meet the demands of Augustus for his palace. It was an easy task for the modellers to create these large pieces, but a great problem for the kiln-masters to fire them (some were over four feet high); in consequence the excessive shrinkage often resulted in fire-cracks. On rare occasions they were subjected to further kiln-firings to fuse enamel colours, but, in most cases only unfired lacquer colours were applied.

Whatever talent Kirchner possessed as a porcelain modeller, it was quickly overshadowed in 1731 by the appointment of the sculptor Johann Joachim Kaendler. Kirchner's animal models, so often a complete fantasy, soon gave way to Kaendler's natural forms. Not content to confine his talents to figures, Kaendler's influence was soon seen on the many practical wares, and the brilliant painting introduced by J. G. Herold was forced to give way to pieces decorated in the so-called "plastic" style with high relief modelling.

Augustus the Strong died in 1733, two years after Kaendler's appointment. His son, who acceded to the Polish throne as Augustus III, was more interested in pictures than porcelain and, consequently, his ambitious minister Count Heinrich von Brühl was appointed as Director, a post he held for thirty years. Kaendler's early influence is best seen on the famous

"Swan Service" that was produced between 1737 and 1741 for Count Brühl and consisted of several hundred pieces. The swan was the main theme and, when set out, the whole service was intended to suggest a water show, with low relief swans being modelled on all the practical wares, while nereids, dolphins and tritons acted as supports for the smaller shell dishes and tazzas. The table would be further decorated with mirrors and green paper to simulate the water. Many of these pieces are known to be the work of the modeller J. F. Eberlein (d. 1749) who worked under Kaendler's direction from 1735. An earlier, but less well-known, service was made in 1735 for Count Sulkowsky, having another relief pattern which enjoyed long popularity: the *Ozier* pattern, a basket-work design used mostly on the rims of plates from about 1732. There were many different varieties of this new fashion and many other similar relief border patterns, including palms, scrolls, flowers and shells. Such monumental pieces of porcelain are essentially museum pieces and the amateur porcelain collector will obviously prefer the smaller figures that can be more easily handled and appreciated. By 1740 Kaendler was modelling a profusion of figures, such as actors and actresses from the Italian Comedy, elegant ladies, peasants, street-criers, sportsmen and their companions and a host of other superbly modelled characters (Pl. 8B).

Visitors who attended banquets at the Dresden Court could not fail to be impressed by the lavish table decorations and in 1748 Sir Charles Hanbury-Williams, who at the time was the British Ambassador at the Court of Augustus III, attended a dinner where an eight-foot-high porcelain fountain flowed with rose-water.

Kaendler's best models were produced during the height of the vogue for Baroque styles and consequently the majority of his figures remain unmarred by the extravagant Rococo scroll-work bases that soon followed. The modelling is vigorous and the enamel colours strong and pure. Although much use was made of the popular oriental style flower painting on the ladies' ample skirts and on the breeches of the gallants, it was rarely that the enamels did not permit a reasonable amount of the pure white porcelain to shine through and remind one of the fragile material. One can scarcely associate early Kaendler modellers with the general idea of pretty Dresden figures; in fact his satirical figures appear almost brutally ugly.

Even the beautiful hard-paste porcelain of Meissen was liable to warp at peak kiln-temperatures and so, inevitably, tree stumps or pedestals were necessary to support the male characters with their slender stockinged legs; the ladies, with their long full gowns were self-supporting. It is worthwhile noting that figures painted in the earlier years of Meissen, tend to have this additional bulk of clay left white, whereas later, and especially in the nineteenth century, it is fully painted to represent a naturalistic tree-stump or marble pedestal.

Many of the late nineteenth-century porcelains painted in imitation of Meissen, show the style of painting that had been popular in about 1740. In 1741 the factory had acquired large stocks of French engravings that were, undoubtedly, a great source of inspiration for a new painting style influenced by the work of such artists as Watteau, Boucher, and Teniers. These scenes of pastorals, peasants and *putti*, with their typical asymmetrical scrollwork frames, also herald the arrival of Rococo at Meissen.

By the mid-eighteenth century the Meissen factory was employing over five hundred workers and exporting large quantities of its wares to such places as Russia, Turkey, England, Poland and France, but this period of prosperity was to be short-lived, for in 1756 the state of Saxony became involved in the Seven Years War. The country was invaded by the troops of Frederick the Great of Prussia and the factory was occupied. The only major customer during these years was Frederick himself, who had many pieces made at the factory as gifts for his friends. Many of the foremost workers left the country and some who found employment in other porcelain factories never returned. Such was the case of the modeller Elias Meyer who had been engaged to replace Eberlein in 1748. He was a much younger man than Kaendler and easily adapted his modelling style to the now popular Rococo fashions, whereas Kaendler, who had grown up in the age of Baroque, found the transition much more difficult (Pl. 8B). Meyer was persuaded by Frederick to work in Berlin where, together with his brother, he created the finest figures made at that factory.

In 1763 the war ended, but within months both Augustus III and Count Brühl died and in order to compete with the many other German porcelain factories that had been established in the middle of the century, the Meissen factory was completely re-organized. Despite this, however, its position as the fashionable pace-maker for European porcelain was lost, for everyone now looked towards the Royal factory at Sèvres for inspiration.

In 1764 the Court Painter C. W. E. Dietrich was employed as artistic director. This period, 1763–1774, is generally termed the Academic Period; about this time a dot was placed between the hilts of the crossed-swords mark, hence the more common name of "dot period". Meissen now became almost entirely dependent for its styles upon the flourishing French factory, but their hard-paste had little in common with such beautiful soft-pastes as were produced at Sèvres at this time. Even the French sculptor Michel-Victor Acier was engaged to work in the new, rather sentimental styles, entirely independent of the now ageing Kaendler who died in 1775. His life's ambition, to produce an enormous equestrian figure of Augustus III in porcelain, was never fulfilled. Upon the death of Dietrich in 1774 the Count Camillo Marcolini was appointed sole director of the factory, and a new phase was entered that was to continue as the "Marconi Period" until 1814. During this time the "dot" in the factory mark was often replaced with a star or asterisk, made up of two or three strokes (Pl. 8A).

During both these post-war periods, large stocks of earlier seconds, or faulty wares, were sold off in an effort to recapture some of the lost markets, but the flooding of the market with inferior wares only tended to further lower their reputation. An additional difficulty for the Meissen factory was the popularity of Josiah Wedgwood's cream coloured earthenware that was loudly praised and much purchased throughout Europe.

Apart from the *Louis Seize* and Neo-classical styles of Sèvres, Meissen also drew ideas from the Berlin factory and many of the flower and bird paintings of the late 1760s and 1770s, from both concerns, are almost identical and can be separated only by their marks that are fortunately, almost always, clearly present.

The *Mosaik,* or scale-pattern, which was introduced in about 1760, remained fashionable for many years but the attempts to copy the beautifully coloured grounds of Sèvres were never successful, mainly because of the difference in the glazes; the soft-glaze of Sèvres tended to absorb and soften such colours as the famous *bleu du roi.*

Towards the end of the eighteenth century the director of Meissen, once again, looked elsewhere for new styles, and many services were made with portraits, silhouettes, copies of oil-paintings and sentimental scenes (e.g. from the Sorrows of Werther) painted within gilt frames of ribbons and flowers. Even the over-decorated fashions of Sorgenthal's Vienna were adopted, which resulted in the fatal mistake of hiding completely the white porcelain under a mass of such enamel decoration as "marbling" or the imitation of wood (*décor bois*). Apart from the above-mentioned pieces, great quantities of blue and white wares were still produced featuring the "onion pattern", the "aster pattern", etc. (Pl. 8A).

The majority of Meissen figures on the market today are those made towards the middle of the nineteenth century when Ernst August Leuteritz was in charge of the modelling. Although they were invariably cast from the original moulds, their poor decoration and later colours condemn them as inferior copies of the original eighteenth-century examples.

In 1864 the Meissen factory moved from Albrechtsburg to a new building, erected by the state, at Triebischtal, near the town of Meissen. For several years after the move the bulk of their output still comprised reproductions of old models.

After World War I some very fine figures were modelled by Paul Scheurich, who had previously worked at Berlin. They were a completely new adaptation of the old styles, his subject matter being mostly Chinese, theatrical or classical. Meissen still produces many table-wares of their more modest eighteenth-century styles, but the fine white porcelain has now given way to a very poor greyish material.

It is fitting, at this point, to consider the many minor, eighteenth- and nineteenth-century concerns that benefited from the fame of the original factory. When the management of Meissen published "The Festive Publication" in 1910, to commemorate their two hundredth anniversary, they listed seventeen factories employing marks "which can be confounded with those of the Royal Manufactory in Meissen".

The most common mark to appear on Meissen copies is that of Alfred Voigt, of Sitzendorf, who used two parallel lines with a third stroke through the centre at an angle. Samson of Paris used two cross-strokes with a third across; Carl Thieme of Potschappel (Pl. 9B) a cross and "T" and many others. Samson should not be accredited with the cross and "S" that was the mark of Eduard Liebermann of Schney. Even many of the Dresden decorators adopted similar, confusing marks, for example, F. Hirsch used a cross and "H". Also illustrated in Pl. 9B is a copy of a figure from the famous monkey band, originally modelled by Kaendler. In this case, however, it is the work of Ernst Bohne of Rudolstadt, Thuringia, and borrows the mark of the crowned "N" which was first used at the Royal Naples Factory in 1771.

Major German Porcelain Factories

For many years the Meissen factory enjoyed almost sole monopoly of hard-paste porcelain manufacture in Europe. But as the middle years of the century were reached, more work-men who had acquired knowledge at Meissen became prepared to sell this information, with the result that porcelain manu-factures soon appeared in many other German states. The first of these factories was established at Höchst in 1746, although they had very little success before 1750.

Höchst
Adam Friedrich von Löwenfinck, both a practical potter and decorator, started at Meissen in 1726, then went to Bayreuth, Ansbach, Fulda and Weissenau, arriving in 1746 at Mainz, where he set up a pottery producing tin-glazed earthenware (faience). A privilege for the foundation of a porcelain factory

at Höchst was granted to Löwenfinck, J. C. Göltz and J. F. Clarus in February 1746, but it would appear that Löwenfinck left for Strasbourg in 1749 without having produced any porcelain.

Hard-paste porcelain was eventually produced at Höchst-on-Main in 1750 by Johann Benckgraff and Josef Jakob Ringler, both previously at Vienna. There was constant friction at the factory among the management until the death of Göltz in 1757. The factory was then maintained by the Trustees in Bankruptcy of Mainz until 1759 when the Elector Emmerich Joseph arranged for the factory to be managed by Johann Heinrich Mass, although in 1760 the employees numbered only twenty-five, nine of whom were making faience. Re-organisation was again necessary in 1765 and this time it was placed under a Company of twenty shareholders which included the Elector. After further losses due to declining sales and fierce competition the factory was complately taken over in 1778 by the Elector Friedrich Karl and was eventually closed in 1796.

The earliest wares produced at Höchst had a rather coarse body and a milky-white glaze, but improvements were soon made and, in keeping with the trend in so many similar factories, the emphasis was placed on the production of superb original figures, as well as table-wares. Landscapes, *chinoiserie*, and flower-painting in the Meissen style were all coupled with elaborate Rococo scrollwork frames often showing a preference for deep purples and lavish gilding. One is often conscious that such decoration is by the hand of an artist more accustomed to decorating the thick opaque glaze of earthenware.

Among the earliest and most important figures produced at Höchst are the Italian Comedy models, placed on high, square pedestals. There seems little doubt that both these and the almost identical figures with the mark of Fürstenberg were modelled by craftsmen working from an identical engraving. Opinion is divided as to whether the figures of both factories are the work of Simon Feilner, who produced his models at Höchst with a liveliness reminiscent of the early Kaendler figures and then, working a little later at Fürstenberg, altered his style so much that the models would appear to be the work of different men. The Fürstenberg figures have a detailed fussiness which is far less pleasing and would certainly appear to be the work of another hand, perhaps under the direction of Feilner who was employed there from 1753–54.

Höchst was one of the first factories to produce pastoral groups and Court characters set in front of an arbour, a characteristic of the Chelsea factory during their gold-anchor period. These groups and other similar, slightly pretentious, doll like, figures are usually attributed to the modeller Johann Friedrich Lück.

Laurentius Russinger who was chief modeller at H chst from 1759–67 is credited with slightly larger groups in a "Boucher" manner. He favoured both pastoral and Chinese figures from engravings by Nilson and others, always placed on a green-covered base and occasionally edged with Rococo scrollwork which was far less elaborate than that of Franken-thal.

In 1767 Russinger was succeeded by Johann Peter Melchior, whose earlier work, especially of children, would also appear to have been inspired by Boucher's paintings. The charming antics of children all too soon gave way to more classical sentimentality and such miniature sculptured works as "The Crucifixion" of about 1775. Melchior went to work at Franken-thal in 1779.

When closed in 1796 the moulds passed into the hands of factories at Damm and Bonn, both of whom made faience reproductions of the early models falsely marked as Höchst. In 1904 the moulds were acquired by a firm at Passau, who made some even more dangerous reproductions in porcelain.

From 1750–60 the usual mark on Höchst porcelain is a wheel with between four and eleven spokes; six is the most common, though eight is usual on forgeries. These early marks are either in enamel colour, incised or impressed. A similar mark in underglaze-blue was used from 1760–96 while the addition of an Electoral Hat above the wheel denotes a date between 1760–74.

Fürstenberg

Duke Carl I of Brunswick was highly delighted when in 1747 Johann Christoph Glaser, who claimed to possess all the necessary knowledge and skill to produce porcelain, offered his services. A castle at Fürstenberg was put at his disposal and the excited Duchess Philippine Charlotte threw out all her porcelain under the impression that it could be ground down and formed afresh. The claims of Glaser were false but he somehow managed to engage twenty workmen for the production of faience until 1753 when Benckgraff was persuaded to leave Höchst for Fürstenberg. Benckgraff brought with him the modeller Feilner and the painter, Johannes Zeschinger, but he died before he could contribute more than the most elementary details of the making of porcelain.

W. B. Honey suggests that in order to hide the many imperfections in their clays, vases and table-wares were deliberately designed with rather high relief Rococo scroll-work rather than plain surfaces. Plates of 1758 described as "the plates with eight engraved shields" have intricate fretted borders which suggest the Edwardian souvenirs with a print of the pier. This description can only justifiably relate to the form and certainly not the painting which was often by the hand of Johann Friedrich Metzsch of the Brunswick Academy of Painting.

The earliest figures of Fürstenberg are attributed to Simon Feilner, whose work is discussed under "Höchst". Dr. Ducret points out the unmistakable coarse faces of the ladies with big noses, a stroke of red paint between the lips and chin and the initials "CB" for Caspar Böcker, the Fürstenberg "repairer" or assembler. By 1760 the quality of Fürstenberg porcelain had improved to such an extent that simple plain forms were produced, relying solely upon enamel and gilt decoration of *chinoiserie* after Huquier and Pillement, landscapes in the manner of Watterloo and flower-sprays. During the early 1770s some very fine figures were modelled by J. C. Rombrich, A. C. Luplau, Desoches and C. G. Schubert. The work of the Frenchman, Desoches, has a quality of Niderviller faience, while his lifesize biscuit busts were undoubtedly inspired by Sèvres. Luplau favoured amusing satirical groups such as the lady searching for a flea. Rombrich is generally associated with the amusing and accomplished copies of the famous Meissen *Affenkapelle* or "Monkey Band".

In 1795 the factory was under the management of L. V. Gerverot, who had previously worked at Sèvres and Wedgwood's factory. Gerverot introduced such Neo-classical fashions as black basaltes and biscuit porcelain busts which were followed by the metal forms of the Empire period painted in excess. In 1859 the Fürstenberg factory passed into private hands and is still in operation as a limited liability company.

Varying forms of a cursive "F" in underglaze-blue have been used as a mark since the start of the factory until today, while biscuit porcelain busts have the impressed mark of a running horse.

Berlin

The first factory in Berlin to make hard-paste porcelain had a very short life; established in 1751 by Wilhelm Kaspar

Wegely, a wool merchant, it was forced to close in 1757. Wegely was apparently persuaded to venture into this new trade by the arcanist Benckgraff, from Höchst, who arranged to supply him with the necessary clay. In 1753 Wegely produced his first porcelains with clays from Aue, the same source as Meissen, and King Frederick was apparently so pleased with the results that Wegely was granted many privileges concerning customs duties and taxes. Wegely hoped to obtain skilled workers from the Meissen factory but due to the Seven Years War, which started in 1756, he found the factory almost deserted.

With the help of I. J. Clauce, a painter who may have been at Meissen, and E. H. Reichard as chief modeller, Wegely produced some quite attractive figures of children in various guises with noticeably large heads and long hands on full Rococo bases with close ribbing. The usual mark was "W" in underglaze-blue or impressed, but this letter was also used elsewhere, such as at Wallendorf.

When Wegely's factory closed Reichard continued to produce wares alone until in 1761 he was approached by a financier, J. E. Gotzkowski, who was prepared to support the establishment of a large factory. Gotzkowski enlisted the aid of such people as the Meissen modeller F. E. Meyer, K. W. Böhme a landscape painter, J. Borrmann who specialized in painting battle-scenes and K. J. C. Klipfel a flower-painter. By 1762 Gotzkowski, employing many workers who had been at the Meissen factory and having complete staff numbering about 150, still showed a financial loss, with the result the factory was purchased in 1763 by Frederick the Great and is still State owned. The porcelain produced at Berlin is considered to have been at its best during the life of Frederick, who died in 1786. Many fine services were produced for the King, most of which were decorated with *Mosaik* or scale-pattern borders, a type of decoration in which Klipfel specialized. It is

Above (Pl. 9A), figure of a girl, hard-paste porcelain in enamel colours. After a model by J. G. Müller. Mark, a sceptre in underglaze-blue. German, *c.* 1780. Ht: 4⅞ in.; group of a man and girl, hard-paste porcelain in enamel colours. After model by K. G. Lück. Mark, 'CT' monogram under a crown in underglaze-blue. German (Frankenthal), *c.* 1770–75. Ht: 6 in.; figure of Arion, hard-paste porcelain in enamel colours. After model by J. C. W. Beyer. German (Ludwigsburg), *c.* 1760. Ht: 5⅝ in. *Below* (Pl. 9B), figure of a monkey, hard-paste porcelain in enamel colours. Mark, a crowned 'N' in underglaze-blue. German (Thuringian), 20th century. Ht: 5 in.; plate, hard-paste porcelain in enamel colours. Mark, shield with arms of Hungary in blue enamel. Hungarian (Herend), *c.* 1850. Diam: 8¼ in.; candlestick, hard-paste porcelain in enamel colours. Mark, shield and 'Dresden' in blue enamel. German (Potschappel, Carl Thieme), 20th century. Ht: 8 in.

Above (Pl. 10A), jar and cover, soft-paste porcelain in enamel colours. Mark, 'DCP' incised. French (Mennecy), mid-18th century. Ht: $6\frac{3}{8}$ in.; plate, soft-paste porcelain in underglaze blue. Mark, hunting-horn and 'Chantilly' in blue. French (Chantilly), *c.* 1750–60. Diam: $9\frac{1}{2}$ in.; cup and saucer, soft-paste porcelain. French (Saint-Cloud), first half of 18th century. Diam of saucer: $4\frac{7}{8}$ in. *Below* (Pl. 10B), figure of Chinese, soft-paste porcelain in enamel colours. French (probably Mennecy), *c.* 1740. Ht: $7\frac{3}{4}$ in.; group of children, soft-paste porcelain in enamel colours. French (Mennecy), *c.* 1755. Ht: $6\frac{5}{8}$ in.

difficult today to judge comparative values, but a simple example shows that Meyer, the chief modeller, received a salary of 2,000 talers, while "The green Potsdam" table service cost 7,646 talers.

The majority of the Berlin table-wares show a preference for far more simplified versions of Rococo than those used at Meissen, sometimes including distinctly English styles, and providing large plain surfaces which lent themselves to boldly painted decoration in a palette which included a bright orange red, greys and rose-pinks.

The figures produced at Berlin during this same period were nearly all modelled by Friedrich and Wilhelm Meyer and lovers of porcelain figures may well criticize them as being as large as sculpture. Wilhelm's groups particularly follow the pyramid construction of contemporary Neo-classical style sculpture with noticeably small heads and elongated limbs; these similarities are especially apparent when the groups were left in the white glazed state or in the biscuit.

Friedrich Elias Meyer, who came from the Meissen factory in 1761, was succeeded in 1785 by a new master-modeller Johann Georg Müller. Müller also modelled some rather large compositions but his grouping may best be described as awkward as he forced his characters into unnatural poses (Pl. 9A).

During the late eighteenth and early nineteenth century Berlin tended to leave many of their wares in the biscuit state especially when in Neo-classical styles. The Berlin wares most likely to be seen by the amateur collector are the "porcelain pictures": flat slabs of porcelain enamelled with copies of famous paintings from National collections with signatures which can rarely be traced to a recorded painter, and lithophanies, the thinly moulded panels of biscuit-porcelain which when held to the light reveal a black-and-white picture; these generally have the impressed "KPM" mark (*Königliche*

5

Porzellan-Manufaktur). The nineteenth-century factories of Henneberg and Plaue used similar marks of "HPM" and "PPM" on their own lithophanies.

Nymphenburg

Today the figures produced at Nymphenburg in Bavaria in about 1755 are as popular with collectors as those of early Meissen; their price, however, is now unfortunately within the range of very few.

Although earlier experiments justify a starting date of 1747, it was not until the arrival of the nomadic arcanist Ringler in 1753, that true porcelain of a quality comparable to that of Meissen was manufactured. In 1754 Franz Anton Bustelli arrived at the factory to take charge of the modelling, and it is through his work that this Bavarian factory has achieved such a high reputation. Bustelli is thought to have died in 1763, but as his name was a fairly common one in that area there is some doubt whether this accepted date is correct.

The factory was first situated in a mansion at Neudeck, near Munich, and moved to a building adjacent to the Palace of Nymphenburg in 1761. Between 1755–67 the manufactory enjoyed the patronage of Prince Max III Joseph of Bavaria and, although running at a loss, it managed to produce wares superior to any other German porcelain of the time.

In the short period Bustelli was modelling at Nymphenburg, he accomplished a great deal; his subjects cover a multitude of types, all modelled as if carved from wood, often in the manner of the sculptor Ignaz Günther. Crucifixion figures, gallants, various hawkers, ardent lovers, groups of Chinese figures, seasons and most of all, his familiar Italian Comedy figures, were all modelled with the same twisting motion of the hips, helping to give an interesting viewpoint from almost any angle. Bustelli probably more than any other modeller used the spirit of Rococo to advantage on his bases, replacing the inevitable tree stump or pedestal so necessary to support the figures in the initial kiln firing, with a rising crest-like support, almost like a wave. His choice of colouring, especially on the Italian Comedy figures, was always pleasing, while a preference for striped material tends to emphasize the movement of the characters.

Bustelli was succeeded in 1763 by Dominikus Auliczek, the man who is wrongly credited with the modelling of almost every group of fighting animals in existence. He is in fact considered to be actually responsible for only about twenty-five such groups, which must have been popular decorations for Bavarian hunting-lodges.

In addition to figures, Nymphenburg also produced excellent table-wares, some of which are considered to have been modelled by Bustelli himself; the strong similarity between some of the tureen handles and the Rococo bases of the figures would certainly favour this suggestion.

The gay life at the Munich Court called for lavish table-pieces which were kept in the stores of the court confectioners. These services were usually decorated with flowers, fruit, birds or landscapes, and early enamel art-work was often slightly faulty so that such colours as the blues and greens tended to flake off.

The usual mark of Nymphenburg has always been an impressed chequered shield, although this shape differed over the years, or alternatively a hexagram (Star of David) in underglaze-blue.

The factory was run by the State until 1862 when it was taken over by a private company. It still makes high quality reproductions of many early models and the figures tend to be of a creamier-coloured porcelain with hollow, rather than flat bases.

Frankenthal

Having failed to obtain the permission of King Louis XV of France to continue his porcelain manufacture at Strasbourg, Paul Hannong chose to take his knowledge across the Rhine to Frankenthal, where the Elector Carl Theodor permitted him to settle in some old barrack buildings. Towards the end of 1755, within only eight months of his arrival, Hannong was producing wares of sufficiently high quality to be presented as gifts to Court Ambassadors. When the factory was well established Paul Hannong returned to Strasbourg, leaving his elder son, Charles-François-Paul, in charge as director. Charles died in 1757 and his younger brother, Joseph Adam, then took over and in 1759 purchased the factory from his father, who died the following year. In 1762 the factory was purchased by the Elector, Carl Theodor.

Despite the high quality of the wares and figures made for the remainder of the century the factory was finally closed in 1800, the moulds going to such places as Grünstadt and Nymphenburg, where they were later used to make reproductions of the earlier Frankenthal models.

The porcelain made from a Passau clay, was of a very high standard and as can be expected, the extravagant Rococo of Strasbourg faience again appears in this new venture of Hannong's. The early figures were modelled by J. W. Lanz. They tend to be of a slightly smaller scale than elsewhere, have distinctly small heads and were placed in theatrical poses, with grass-covered bases edged with gilt Rococo scrollwork.

J. L. Lück is attributed with the modelling of slightly later figures, as illustrated on Pl. 9A, in much the same spirit as those of Lanz. The figures in his groups have a much healthier and robust appearance and his bases are usually higher with extreme Rococo scrollwork, often pierced. Use was often made of arbours, fashioned from either trellises or more Rococo scrollwork.

The Court-sculptor Linck was associated with the factory models for many years. As can be expected from a sculptor, his compositions were rather over-dramatic for the scale and the medium, sometimes taking the form of a complete opera scene depicting several characters. In about 1765 Karl Gottlieb Lück, the brother of the aforementioned J. L. Lück, succeeded Linck as model-master and although he had been a pupil of Kaendler, at Meissen, his compositions show no trace of the master, for despite the outstanding craftsmanship, they have a quality of prettiness and fussiness with over-extravagant colouring.

By the time Adam Bauer arrived at Frankenthal (1777) the fashion of Rococo was past and, to keep up with the popular trend, he produced figures of a classical nature but his voluptuous studies of such characters as Venus have little relationship with antiquity. Bauer was succeeded by J. P. Melchior, who merely continued to produce similar groups to those he had previously modelled at Höchst.

The table-wares of Frankenthal are without doubt closer to the styles of Sèvres than any other German factory. It is not usual to be able to identify the hand of the painter on such pieces, but at Frankenthal, due to signed documentary examples, it is possible to suggest Winterstein (1758–81) as the painter of subjects after Teniers, Osterspey (1759–82) can be associated with mythology, and Johann Bernard Magnus with battle-scenes.

The usual mark of Frankenthal is "CT" for Carl Theodor, in monogram form under an electoral crown. A few early wares bear the impressed "PH" (Paul Hannong) or "PHF" (Paul Hannong Frankenthal) while a rather more rare mark is "JAH" (Joseph-Adam Hannong), together with a crowned lion rampant.

Ludwigsburg

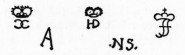

Johann Jakob Ringler's final contribution to the history of German porcelain was at Ludwigsburg, where in 1758 he established a factory for Duke Carl Eugen of Württemberg. He had put his knowledge of the techniques of hard-paste porcelain manufacture into practice at something like seven different centres, but having reached Ludwigsburg he was apparently tired of his travels, for he remained there until his death in 1802. The Duke poured a great deal of money into his factory and it is recorded in 1766 that 154 workers were employed, although about half of their wages were paid in factory "wasters" which they in turn had to sell. Following the death in 1793 of Duke Carl, the factory rapidly declined until the final closure in 1824.

The paste of Ludwigsburg porcelain is probably easier to identify than that of any other German factory. The colour is a distinct smoky-brown as if it had been discoloured by kiln-fumes (similar to some early Plymouth wares), but the exquisite detail in the figures suggests that it was an ideal clay for modelling.

As with so many of the German factories, the table-wares of Ludwigsburg show very little originality. The only person who really warrants attention was G. F. Riedel, for he not only painted but also designed some very fine vases with Rococo scrollwork in low relief. Riedel was chief designer to the factory from 1759–79 and was responsible initially for figures as well as practical wares.

Duke Carl's great interest was ballet (J. G. Neverre the famous dance theorist, was employed at the Court of Württemberg) and this is reflected in some of the earliest Ludwigsburg groups of dancers which are attributed to the factory's chief "repairer", Jean Louis. There are many coarse reproductions of these figures usually on dull flat bases instead of the lively Rococo of the originals. J. J. Louis was also responsible for modelling some delightful miniature groups. Despite being exceptionally small (the paved bases are usually only about 3in. by 2in.), these "Venetian Fairs" manage to portray such scenes as inns, tailor's shops, booksellers, etc., including several figures with every detail carefully modelled. The Duke is thought to have suggested "Venetian Fairs" as a theme for a court festival after visiting Venice in 1767.

J. C. W. Beyer was apparently responsible for many of the "lean and hungry" looking figures made at the factory from about 1760, although he was not put in charge of the workshop until 1764. The figure illustrated on Pl. 9A is typical of the many figures produced during the 1760s of rather humble subjects, peasants, hawkers, beggars, etc.

It is less easy to identify with such certainty the work of other modellers known to have been at Ludwigsburg. J. C. Haselmeyer, formerly a court confectioner, is thought to have been responsible for some beautifully composed groups of about 1780.

Johann Göz, (chief "repairer" 1760–2) is thought to have modelled at least thirty of the finest figures produced at the factory; but the only one now thought to be in this country is of an actor and is in the Cecil Higgins Museum, Bedford.

Pierre François Lejeune and Domenico Ferretti were both court sculptors who are known to have produced models for porcelain figures; but apart from the very regal "Chinese ballet" figures attributed without very good reason to the latter, their work is almost impossible to identify.

The most common mark seen on Ludwigsburg porcelain is two back to back interlaced "C's", below a ducal crown. When Duke Ludwig succeeded Duke Carl in 1793 the "C's" were replaced by "L" and from 1796–1816, an "FR" monogram for King Frederick. In 1816 Frederick was succeeded by William, with the resulting "WR" monogram. Three stag's horns in a shield, from the arms of Württemberg, were sometimes used in the years around 1800.

Minor German Porcelain Factories

Ansbach

Johann Frederick Kaendler, possibly a relative of the famous Meissen modeller, is thought to have been responsible for assisting the Margrave Alexander of Brandenburg to establish a porcelain factory at Ansbach in 1758 which survived until 1860. Very few original ideas seem to have been introduced at this factory. Fine quality table-wares with superb painting tended to follow the fashions set by Meissen, Berlin and Nymphenburg, although some of the rarer *chinoiserie* pieces show originality at least in the use of scenes taken from illustrations in seventeenth-century travel-books.

A great awareness of Berlin work is apparent in the majority of Ansbach figures, especially a series depicting various gods, but the typical Ansbach features are present in the light weight, elongated bodies, and the familiar half-closed eyes painted in red. Other interesting groups inspired by plays written by the wife of the Margrave Alexander show groups of lovers, hunters or allegories set against architectural arbours.

When marked, figures have an impressed shield of the arms of Ansbach showing a stream with three fishes. The more common mark on practical wares is an underglaze-blue "A", either alone, with a shield as mentioned above, or under a Prussian eagle.

Kelsterbach

The first period of porcelain manufacture at Kelsterbach

(1761–68) was surprisingly productive for such a brief space of time. The Landgrave of Hesse-Darmstadt, Ludwig VIII, obtained the services of the arcanist C. D. Busch in 1761. Busch was apparently more successful with his experiments than he had been elsewhere. His previous attempts to prove himself a skilled arcanist at Bayreuth and Sèvres having proved disappointing. There are at least seventy-five different models attributed to the modeller Carl Vogelmann, although many are taken from identical moulds and it is only clever assembly work which has produced so many different poses. Vogelmann's approach to Rococo is considered as one of the most attractive; some of his models are so rare that they may well have been modelled directly in the semi-hard clay rather than by moulding, a suggestion borne out by the lack of seam marks, so often apparent along the limbs of the figures.

According to contemporary factory inventories, no large services were made at Kelsterbach during the first period and, apart from the usual range of smaller table-wares, their speciality would appear to have been such "toys", as snuff-boxes, scent-bottles, cane-handles, etc. The rather rare mark was "HD" under a crown in underglaze-blue. Porcelain was again made at Kelsterbach from 1789–92, and it was during this period that the larger services of table-wares were produced.

Ottweiler

Prince Wilhelm Heinrich of Nassau-Saarbrücken was well-known for his interest in the arts and the well-being of his people. Therefore when he established a porcelain factory in 1764, he made himself personally responsible for the hiring of Etienne-Dominique Pellevé, a painter and potter from Rouen, together with G. H. J. Wagner as technical director. Pellevé was apparently a difficult man to work with as Wagner left a year later and Grahl, a painter from Dresden, left the factory in 1769, complaining about the Frenchman in charge; Paul-Louis Cyfflé worked at Ottweiler for only a short while in about 1765, before leaving for similar reasons.

Wilhelm Heinrich was succeeded in 1765 by his son Ludwig, who in 1769 leased the factory to R. F. Jolly and N. Leclerc. Further French modellers and painters were engaged in producing porcelain until 1789, when the entire concern was devoted to making glazed English-style earthenware, production of which had started in 1784. The factory was finally closed in 1794 due to the French Wars.

Ottweiler porcelain is rare and consequently difficult to identify, especially when it is not marked with "N.S." in either underglaze-blue or gold (for "Nassau-Saarbrücken"). The best wares were made between 1764 and 1770. The tablewares are usually in popular Rococo styles with landscapes, mythological or Italian Comedy scenes often painted in purple monochrome within a frame of gilt scrollwork. Further features include the preference for square-sectioned handles and the distinctive grey body of the paste which was noticeable from about 1768, when the Passau kaolin originally in use was replaced by clays from Tholy.

Fulda

The porcelain produced at Fulda from 1764–89 was of an exceptionally high quality; possibly the reason for its closure as not being economic. The Prince Bishop of Fulda, Heinrich VIII, first established the factory with the aid of Nikolaus Paul, the arcanist from Weesp.

The Fulda table-wares are usually in a simplified, but elegant, form of Rococo, while the painting tended to follow the Meissen styles with a preference for an iron-red monochrome. But it is the figures of Fulda which are preferred by collectors.

Many of the finest figures of Fulda are attributed to the

modeller and sculptor Wenzel Neu who had previously worked at Sitzendorf and Kloster-Veilsdorf. Many other Fulda models which follow show a distinct similarity to those of Frankenthal, and are thought to have been the work of the modeller Georg Bartholomei, who came from Ansbach to Fulda in 1771, remaining until his death in 1778. In *German Porcelain* Dr. S. Ducret points out that if Bartholomei is to be accepted as the modeller of the elegant series of Fulda musicians, he must have altered his earlier style considerably as they show no relation to the chubby *putti* said to be by his hand at Ansbach.

The particular interest of some of the Fulda Italian Comedy figures is that they can be identified with the engravings by Jacques Callot, who completed his *Balli di Sfessania* in Nancy in 1622. The mound bases with the inevitable tree-stump support are completely painted over in natural colours, a fashion which would normally suggest a later date than 1780 when most of the series are thought to have been produced.

Several marks were used at Fulda from about 1765–80, the most common being a simple cross. Between about 1780 and 1788 two script "F's" are drawn in such a manner as to suggest "H" for Heinrich, the two "F's" stand for *Fürstlich-Fuldaisch*; this *Heinrichmarke* is drawn under an electoral hat. Finally from about 1788 until about 1790 the "F's" are tipped against each other to form an "A" indicating Prince Heinrich's successor Adalbert.

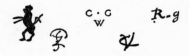

Cassel

The services of the arcanist Nikolaus Paul were similarly obtained by the Landgrave of Hesse-Cassel, Friedrich II, to establish a porcelain factory in Cassel in 1766. Within a very short space of time nine key workers had been persuaded to leave factories of repute and work at the new undertaking which ran until 1788 when, despite continual financial aid from the Prince, the factory was forced to close.

The body, glaze and modelling of the practical wares produced at Cassel were of a low standard. The poor body was probably due to endeavouring to use local clays which resulted in a high percentage of "wasters", while the relief Rococo, picked out in purple enamel, shows a loose and broken style completely lacking the continuous rhythm of true Rococo.

Cassel made many models of such themes as the Months and the Senses, usually enacted by robust little *putti*. These are sometimes marked with an incised worker's mark in addition to the two-tailed lion-rampant from the arms of Hesse, or the "H.C." for Hesse-Cassel.

Pfalz-Zweibrücken

The factory established by J. M. Stahl and Laurentius Russinger at Gutenbrunn in 1767 was moved to Zweibrücken in 1769. Despite the financial aid of Duke Christian IV the factory was forced to close in 1775.

According to the records approximately forty different models of figures are known to have been made at Pfalz-Zweibrücken, and of these only fourteen have been identified, almost all without factory marks. Some of the figures modelled by Russinger are obviously repeats of some of his earlier work when at Höchst; though many of the groups made in the 1770s have a crudity which can well be compared with early nineteenth-century Staffordshire earthenware groups. The mound-like bases were decorated by the simple technique of lightly dabbing colours on with a sponge. The table-wares show little originality in shape, but they were often decorated with very pleasing landscapes, attributed to K. F. Wohlfahrt, in simplified Rococo frames.

Würzburg

A further short-lived factory was established in 1775 by J. C. Geiger at Würzburg, enjoying a privilege from Franz Ludwig von Ertal, Prince-Bishop of Würzburg. The body and glaze, in common with several of the later factories, is of poor quality, an unmistakable feature being an unglazed margin at the base of the wares which is much more of a Far Eastern characteristic. The figures of Würzburg have a naivety which is nevertheless pleasing and characters from the same mould appear in different compositions. Some of the larger and more ambitious groups, such as the Continents, would appear to have been modelled directly in the porcelain paste. Three different types of bases appear to have been used: Rococo, a simple mound and a pile of rocks like those seen on late Italian groups. The mark of these rare examples is "C.G." over "W" for "Casper Geiger Würzburg".

Kloster-Veilsdorf

Since the middle of the eighteenth century the forest region of Thuringia has attracted many porcelain manufacturers, with the result that as one has to be content with merely attributing so many unidentified English wares to Staffordshire, so many of the unmarked German hard-paste porcelains must be grouped under the general heading of "Thuringian".

One of the best-known factories in this area is that established by Prince Friedrich Wilhelm Eugen von Hildburg-hausen in 1760 at Kloster-Veilsdorf. Many well-known workers from other established factories were employed including Abraham Ripp, a kiln worker, Nikolaus Paul, the arcanist, Caspar Schumann, a painter, and Wenzel Neu, the modeller. The employment of so many specialists is reflected in the excellent practical wares produced which were always tastefully decorated by such painters as Döll.

Wenzel Neu is the modeller most likely to have produced the early Kloster-Veilsdorf figures made from about 1760–65; these pieces are of rather inferior quality but typical of the Thuringian wares in general. In about 1780 the four Continents were modelled in an Allegorical style, breaking away from all the usual compositions and costumes. These groups were probably modelled by Kotta who also produced an excellent bust of Prince Friedrich, the founder of the factory. The mark of Kloster-Veilsdorf is composed of varying forms of "CV" (Closter-Veilsdorf), sometimes in monogram form, sometimes with a shield of arms between the two letters and occasionally deliberately drawn to look like the Meissen crossed-swords. The factory was purchased in 1797 by the sons of Gotthelf Greiner who continued to use the same clover-leaf mark as used at their Limbach factory.

Gotha

Wilhelm Theodor von Rothberg is thought to have established the Gotha porcelain factory in about 1757, although few wares worthy of note appear to have been produced before 1772. In this year von Rothberg leased the factory to three of his workers, Christian Schulz, J. G. Gabel and J. A. Brehm, all painters, who in turn employed other skilled technicians, painters and modellers. In 1804 the factory was leased to Egidius Henneberg whose family continued in possession until 1881, when the concern was taken over by the Simson brothers, making only practical wares. The original porcelain was probably made from Passau clay which resulted in a fine creamy white material; from the time Schulz and his companions took over, the wares acquired a distinct Neo-classical style associated with the Louis XVI period. The early mark was an "R", either in blue or impressed, "R-g" for Rothberg,

"G" for Gotha, and in 1804, when Henneberg took over, the name Gotha appears on a strap around a hen. The very late marks of Simson are "Gotha" or "S" within a shield.

Limbach

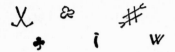

Before he established his porcelain factory, Gotthelf Greiner already owned a glass-works. He must have been a man of exceptional technical knowledge in his time as he apparently perfected his material entirely without the aid of workmen from earlier established factories and within a short time he was employing fifty assistants.

The table-wares are very simple and were obviously made to be sold at a low price. In *German Porcelain*, Dr. Ducret illustrates a Limbach barber's basin which he suggests has more marks than any other piece of porcelain: it bears the painter's name (F. Dressel), the date painted (1778), the owner's mark, the mark of the workshop and the "LB" factory-mark. Many of the figures made in about 1775 bear the mark of crossed-hayforks, another mark intended to confuse the buyer with the crossed-swords of Meissen; these figures are, of course, far below the quality of that factory, but certainly have a simplicity which is none the less pleasing. Unlike the underglaze-blue crossed-swords mark of Meissen, the Limbach marks were applied in either iron-red or purple enamel. This factory still exists.

Ilmenau

The porcelain factory at Ilmenau was established in 1772 by C. Z. Gräbner, but in 1782 it was in such a precarious financial state that it was taken over by the Duke of Weimar, who in turn leased it to Gotthelf Greiner (of Limbach) in 1786. The factory changed hands again in 1792, this time to Christian Nonne. In 1808 Nonne and his son-in-law Roesch purchased the factory which continued until 1871 when it was taken over by a company who are still operating today. The early practical wares and figures cannot be identified with any certainty from the mass of other wares being made in Thuringia at the same time, the "I" in blue being too rare a mark to help to any degree. Between about 1792 to 1808 the factory would appear to have specialized in producing Wedgwood-style plaques in porcelain as compared with the original jasper-ware. Similar contemporary portraits, classical and mythological figures and events were modelled in the familiar blue and white biscuit.

Grossbreitenbach

The porcelain factory of Grossbreitenbach is another Thuringian factory which has continued in production from its establishment in 1777 until the present day. Started by Ernst von Hopfgarten in 1777, the factory was taken over after five years by Greiner of Limbach, who ran the factory more or less as a subsidiary of his Limbach establishment; consequently there are few pieces which can be attributed to Grossbreitenbach with any certainty. The main output would seem to have been of wares decorated in underglaze-blue. The mark, when used, was the same trefoil or three-leaf clover as used at Limbach.

Volkstedt

Upon discovering how to produce a soft-paste porcelain G. H. Macheleid approached Prince Johann Friedrich zu Schwarzburg-Rudolstadt in 1760 and was granted all the privileges he requested to aid him in his venture. In a short time Macheleid succeeded in producing the usual type of German hard-paste porcelain. In 1767 the factory again changed hands and was leased to Christian Nonne, a merchant who guided the concern through nearly thirty years of prosperity until 1793, when it was sold to the state. The factory is still in existence today after numerous nineteenth-century owners.

Volkstedt is better known for its figures than practical wares and at least ninety different models are recorded. As at Kloster-Veilsdorf, many groups were made up by using the same models in various guises: one large recorded group having seven characters, some of which are known as single figures or as part of a pair. Many of the figures were probably intended to portray living Court personages. This is certainly the case with some of the portrait medallions modelled by Franz Kotta and produced in biscuit porcelain about 1785.

Volkstedt was fortunate in being able to use the arms of Schwarzburg-Rudolstadt as its mark, for if carelessly drawn the crossed hayforks can so easily be mistaken for the crossed-swords. On occasions a single hayfork or "R" was used.

Wallendorf

A further factory which has continued from mid-eighteenth century until the present day is that of Wallendorf. The factory was first set up by four men, including Gotthelf Greiner, in 1763. Greiner left for Limbach in 1772 and the factory remained in the possession of the Hamman family until 1829, when it was first leased, and eventually purchased, by F. C. Hutschenreuter. It is still in existence.

Many well-known workers from Thuringian factories are recorded as having worked at Wallendorf during the early years, and since the original records have survived it is possible to accurately attribute many figures to the modeller Gabriel Klein, who is also well-known as the modeller of many Zürich figures. Wallendorf had a large output of both practical wares and figures, records show that in 1799 as many as 53,000 decorated beakers were exported to Turkey. In about 1770 some interesting groups were made copying earlier bronzes with a certain amount of artistic licence. In such groups the rather early use of bases painted to imitate marble, appears.

With modellers and painters changing from one Thuringian factory to another, it is very difficult to attribute the many unmarked figures from this factory with any degree of accuracy. Three varying bases are seen at Wallendorf: high Rococo picked out in purple, naturalistic earthy mounds with stumps and the simple high, square Neo-classical base. The simple mark of "W" was used from about 1778, but this too is sometimes drawn with the intention of making it look like crossed-swords.

Rauenstein

When seeking to buy German porcelain, the collector will frequently be confronted by wares made at the factory of Rauenstein. The factory was started by the Greiner family in 1783 and is still operating today. During this entire period the table-wares produced have been rather coarsely made and usually decorated in the dull underglaze-blue patterns first made popular at Meissen. The pattern seen most often is the *Zwiebelmuster* or onion-pattern, a style of decoration copied throughout the Continent. Such wares were obviously in great demand, for at the peak of production the factory employed 124 workers. The late eighteenth-century marks are an "R" and star, or "R-n"; from the nineteenth century crossed "hooks" were added to the "R-n".

Gera

The final Thuringian porcelain factory which should be mentioned is that established at Gera in 1780 by J. G. Ehwaldt and J. G. Gotbrecht. Within a year the factory had run into debt and was taken over by the Greiners who ran the factory as a branch of the Volkstedt establishment until 1782. Since this time a succession of owners have continued the factory to the present day. When identified, by either the "G" or "Gera" some of the wares show some rather painstaking decoration on commemorative or presentation wares showing views, portraits and inscriptions on rather late coloured grounds or the "*décor bois*" (as if wood) discussed under Niderviller.

Vienna

The second European hard-paste porcelain factory was established in Vienna in 1717, although success was not achieved until some two years later. The founder of the factory was Claudius Innocentius Du Paquier, who from 1705 had been an Army contractor in the city of Vienna. Du Paquier had apparently been trying to manufacture true porcelain for several years but was unsuccessful until he persuaded Samuel Stölzel, the kiln-master at the earlier Meissen factory, to work for him. Stölzel, lured by promise of high wages and rich living arrived in Vienna in January 1719, but when these promises were not fulfilled he risked returning to Meissen taking with him the decorator, Johann Gregor Herold.

The name of Christoph Konrad Hunger is frequently mentioned in connection with the establishment at Vienna. He similarly deserted Meissen in 1717 to assist Du Paquier; his claims to be an accomplished arcanist were apparently false, he is best remembered as a highly talented gilder and enameller.

Due to the difficulty of obtaining suitable clays, the earliest attempts to produce a porcelain body and glaze comparable to that of Meissen failed. Stölzel remedied this drawback by managing to acquire clay from Schneeberg, the same source as the Meissen factory; although we do not know how long Meissen permitted this arrangement to continue.

When Stölzel and Herold left Vienna to return to Meissen, they took the added precaution of assuring a warm welcome by smashing Du Paquier's kilns and moulds, ruining the prepared clays and, according to Hunger, stealing his colours, which at that time were superior to those in use at the Saxon factory. Du Paquier recovered from this setback so that by 1724 he was able to boast of "a warehouse full of splendid pieces".

To relieve his financial difficulties Du Paquier ran lotteries with prizes of porcelain, but was eventually forced to sell the factory to the Austrian Empress Maria Theresa in 1744. Du Paquier remained for a short time as director, but then retired on a pension, dying in 1751. In 1783 the factory once again ran into financial difficulties and since no buyer could be found, a successful wool-merchant, Konrad von Sorgenthal, took over as manager and was responsible for bringing to the factory a period of success which lasted well into the nineteenth century. The concern eventually closed in 1866.

The wares produced at Vienna from 1719–44, the "Du Paquier period", have no regular factory-mark; the well-known "two-bar shield", the arms of Austria, was not adopted until 1744, so that certain attribution and dating within this early period are hazardous. As can be expected the early painted decoration tends to be similar to Meissen, the influence of Herold being obvious. Oriental flowers, *chinoiserie*, and early forms of European flowers are all in evidence, the latter being painted in a less naturalistic manner than at the Saxon factory.

Du Paquier specialized in extreme Baroque ornament: scrollwork, shell-like palmettes and intricate lattice-like gilding are invariably present on the borders of dishes, tureens and other fine table-wares. These styles of decoration are attributed to such people as Anton Schulz who later went to Fulda, and Josef Dannhöfer whose work can be documented on Bayreuth faience from 1737.

It is difficult at times to distinguish between pieces of Vienna porcelain of the Du Paquier period decorated at the factory itself, and those decorated by one of the accomplished outside decorators such as Bottengruber or Preissler.

Jacobus Helchis is often considered a decorator of Vienna porcelain although there is no evidence to show that he was actually an employee during the Du Paquier period. However the initials "JH" on a very finely gilded *Jagdservice* (hunting-service) in Vienna are accepted as indicating his work, as are the black-enamelled birds and animals coupled with the Vienna version of the *Laub und Bandelwerk* (leaf and strapwork) borders.

Virtually the only type of figure-modelling carried out at Vienna during the Du Paquier period is in the form of *putti* or Chinese figures used as knops or decoration on the larger pieces of table-services or in the form of handles such as illustrated on Pl. 7B. Further research has recently made possible the attribution of two large white *chinoiserie* figures to the Du Paquier period.

After 1744, when the factory became state-owned, we see less of the finer wares decorated in an individual manner and more of the typical European hard-paste porcelain of the Rococo period. A distinct improvement is noticeable in the colour of the clay. Wares of the early period tend to be smoky-grey in tone while wares bearing the underglaze-blue, impressed, or enamelled shield are distinctly whiter through the substitution of the clay of Passau for a fine quality Hungarian clay.

During the early years of the State period (1744–84) Vienna once more looked towards Meissen rather than Sèvres for their

Rococo styles and indeed many Meissen workmen were persuaded to come to work in Austria. Among the best known of these deserters were Johann Gottfried Klinger, the painter associated with the beautiful naturalistic flower-painting on Meissen (Pl. 8A), J. G. Richter, another flower-painter, Schindler, a painter of snuff-boxes, and J. G. Starcke. The figures made during this period are considerably superior to the rather mediocre table-wares. Once again the earliest figures followed those made at Meissen and included characters from the Italian Comedy series, dwarfs of the "Callot" type and the popular "Dresden" groups of ladies in elaborate dresses, most of which are attributed on rather slight evidence to the "repairer" and modeller Leopold Dannhauser.

From about 1760, a large number of Meissen-type figures were modelled under the direction of the chief modeller J. J. Niedermayer, who was in charge of that department from 1747 until his death in 1784. Shepherds, vendors, waiters, musicians, gallants and mythological and Biblical figures were all produced with a slightly prettier and doll-like quality than the originals. These can be attributed to the early or later part of the period by the bases which start as a mound with a little scrollwork, becoming more like a flat slab a little later, and then moving towards a Neo-classical high base and vertical edging with moulded and gilt designs. Anton Grassi, who succeeded Niedermayer as chief modeller, was responsible for the full Neo-classical treatment of the figures of the Sorgenthal period which followed, many being left "in the biscuit", a current practice at Sèvres.

The wares of the Sorgenthal period (1784–1866) are probably much more familiar to the amateur collector and were copied by very many other factories long after the factory itself closed. The jug illustrated in Pl. 7B is typical of the high quality wares made in the extravagant taste of the time.

In the same manner as Wedgwood in England, Vienna tried

to re-capture the forms of classical antiquity. Perhaps, like Sèvres examples of the same period, they tended to go a little too far with their decoration, for the entire porcelain surface was either lavishly enamelled or gilt to such an extent that one has difficulty in fully appreciating the fragility of the material.

The original work of such artists as Raphael, Piranesi and Angelica Kauffman was often copied, but there must be no confusion here with the late nineteenth- and twentieth-century wares which are signed "Kauffman": these are purely transfer-prints produced by minor Austrian or Bohemian factories or decorators. A useful guide to the recognition of genuine Vienna porcelain after 1783 is, that in addition to the impressed shield, the wares are also impressed with two or three numbers which act as a date-mark, e.g.: 89=1789, 807=1807.

Two people responsible for many imitations of "old Vienna" are Franz Dörfl and Josef Vater who both used a beehive-shaped shield with three and two cross-bars respectively. Many of these late pieces are easily detected by the quality of the gilding alone. The late reproductions can plainly be seen to have had the gilding applied through the application of gold-powder by a rubber-stamp which at times was in-accurately positioned.

Outside Decorators

Hausmaler
In the years immediately following World War II, it was not unusual to see many interesting pieces of Continental porce-lain, such as Meissen, which had been decorated outside the factory by a home decorator. These pieces were perhaps brought to this country by the many refugees from Europe, and today most have found their way into permanent collec-tions and are rarely to be seen, even in the major sale-rooms.

Between 1710, when the Saxon factory of Meissen was

established, and 1728, there was no difficulty in obtaining white-glazed wares, with the result that home decorators came from places as far afield as Holland and Bohemia to purchase these wares so that they themselves might add enamel colours and or gilt to original Meissen forms and sell to their own advantage.

In 1728 the sale of these porcelain "blanks" was forbidden and severe penalties were introduced in order to stop the "botching of enamels and gold". It is suspected that in some cases the artists who were employed at Meissen tried to do a little outside decorating to bolster their poor wages. Despite the ruling, wares were undoubtedly smuggled out of the factory until after the middle of the century, although many of the pieces were outmoded stock. After the Seven Years War (1756–63) large quantities of such pieces were sold off by the factory, who first took the precaution of cancelling out the underglaze-blue factory-mark of crossed-swords by one, two or three cuts through the glaze with the aid of a grinding-wheel. By this time, the day of the finer independent decorators was over and such wares were apparently decorated in minor workshops in poor imitation of earlier true Meissen styles.

The following artists are those whose work is most sought after by collectors today, but such pieces are hard to come by.

Aufenwerth, Johann

Aufenwerth was an Augsburg decorator of Meissen porcelain, working from about 1715 until at least 1728. Pieces signed with the initials "I. A. W." indicate that he generally decorated in silver or gold. His *chinoiserie* designs would appear to have been inspired by the engravings made at Augsburg by Martin Engelbrecht in 1720.

Bottengruber, Ignaz

The Breslau miniature-painter and water-colourist Ignaz

Bottengruber was probably the most accomplished of all porcelain *Hausmaler*. The evidence of signed examples of his work and documents suggest that he was active between 1720–36. As early as 1723 he was using the full enamel palette to produce beautifully painted Bacchanalian scenes surrounded by intricate scrollwork, decorations with military trophies, and battle and hunting scenes. The work of Bottengruber is sometimes confused with his followers, H. G. von Bressler and C. F. von Wolfsburg.

Busch, Canon A. O. E. von dem
The work of Canon Busch of Hildesheim was unique. His designs were engraved into the hard-glaze of Meissen or Fürstenberg porcelain and then black-pigment was rubbed into the engraved lines to show to advantage his preference for ruins, urns, plant-life, animals and figures. The Canon was engraving on both glass and porcelain between about 1748–75. Similar methods were also employed by Canon Kratzberg.

Dannhöfer, Josef Philipp
Dannhöfer is better known as a painter of early Vienna porcelain and there still exists a difference of opinion among authorities as to whether pieces are the work of Dannhöfer during his period at Bayreuth in about 1740, or should be dated slightly earlier to the time when he was working in Du Paquier's factory. Most of the painting attributed to Dannhöfer is in the *chinoiserie* style associated with Herold's early Meissen work.

Ferner, F. J.
The mid-eighteenth-century work of Ferner usually appears on Meissen wares of an earlier date which was originally only decorated in underglaze-blue. His work, which at times mainly consisted of adding enamel colours over the original

design, is of a low quality, his gilding over the blue borders of cups and bowls is similarly of poor quality and is at times much over-done.

Mayer, Franz Ferdinand

It was fortunately the practice of most *Hausmaler* to sign at least some examples of their work. Documentary pieces show that F. F. Mayer was decorating Meissen porcelain between about 1742–51; although the inscribed dates are usually much later than the porcelain which would suggest that he had an arrangement to purchase outmoded or faulty Meissen wares. There are so many examples of work in the style of Mayer that W. B. Honey suggests he may well have had a decorating workshop where others painted under his direction; his own work can sometimes be identified by the appearance of such colours as a light turquoise-green, a dull chocolate-brown and red outlines (Pl. 7B). From 1752–80 similar pastoral and hunting scenes were painted in the more complete enamel palette by his son Franz Mayer.

Meerheim, Johann Gottfried

A painter of early Böttger porcelain from about 1711, using iron-red enamel.

Mehlhorn, Johann Gottfried

Painter of early Böttger porcelain from about 1720, usually of landscapes in iron-red.

Metzsch, Johann Friedrich

Metzsch decorated both oriental and Meissen porcelain at Bayreuth between about 1735–51. His work is often seen on the early form of Böttger cup which has acanthus leaves in relief around the base, as he was apparently able to buy these outmoded pieces long after they had become unfashionable.

He was particularly fond of using continuous landscapes around the entire piece, or masks or baskets of flowers in a Baroque cartouche, and mythological figures.

Preussler, Daniel and Ignaz

Daniel Preussler and his son Ignaz are generally associated with the *Hausmaler* decoration in *Schwarzlot* (black enamel). Such painting on Meissen and Vienna porcelain probably falls within their period 1720–39, the majority of work probably being by Ignaz, as his father died in 1733 at the age of seventy-seven. His early work, often on Chinese porcelain, consists of such scenes as landscapes, seascapes and views of towns. The later Chinese figures in the midst of Baroque scrollwork on Meissen or Vienna porcelain, can sometimes be traced to engravings from Augsburg and are probably the work of Ignaz during his period at Kronstadt (1729–39).

Seuter, Bartholomäus

A silk-dyer from Augsburg who is recorded in 1728 as selling "beautifully decorated porcelain" which he embellished with gold and enamels. Seuter is also known to have painted faience jugs. A single documentary cup signed "Seute" is the only evidence that Seuter also excelled in gilt *chinoiseries*.

Wolfsburg, Carl Ferdinand von

Wolfsburg painted Vienna porcelain as a *Hausmaler* between 1729 and 1748. His style of painting bears out the belief that he was a pupil of Bottengruber, his best work being of mythological scenes painted in purple on plates with borders of gold (*Laub-und-Bandelwerk*), a style more usually seen on *Schwarlot Hausmalerei*.

A good general rule to aid the identification of *Hausmaler* is that the decoration is usually a little too crowded. One gets the feeling that these artists were never able to get sufficient white material for their needs and in consequence kept adding a little more embellishment to the pieces they did manage to acquire.

Switzerland

The porcelains of Switzerland are so rarely seen in England that collectors are inclined to overlook the fine wares produced at Zürich and Nyon.

Zürich

There were no wealthy patrons to subsidize the factory started at Zürich in 1763, but instead a group of businessmen intent upon "making true porcelain, serving their country, and providing bread for needy mouths". The man they hired as technical director, Adam Spengler, was already skilled in the manufacture of faience; he was the father of John James Spengler who modelled at the English Derby factory from 1790–95.

The first porcelain produced at Zürich was a soft-paste similar to that of France, although according to an Austrian who visited the factory in 1764, soapstone was one of the ingredients. After a short while hard-paste porcelain was made using clays from Limoges in France.

The early years of the Zürich factory were apparently very productive, wares were exported to Italy and Holland and records tell of the production of 2,057 pieces within three months during 1764. Apart from innumerable small individual pieces for the table, the factory produced some outstanding services. The most well-known service was made for a Benedictine Monastery (comprising 350 pieces) and is considered one of the finest of its kind to have survived: it was

probably painted by Johannes Daffinger. After the death of
Adam Spengler in 1790 the production of porcelain came to
an end and only rather dull faience was produced.

The sometimes smoky-brown hue of the hard-paste
porcelain has a look comparable to the porcelain of Ludwigsburg; the styles were seldom original, the well-finished,
heavily potted table-wares tending to follow contemporary
German designs.

Salomon Gessner, better known as a poet, is also the best
known painter of the Zürich factory. His work, which can be
identified by signed examples, invariably includes rather
tedious Swiss landscapes, busy with figures, cattle and sheep.

In about 1780 vases were made in the styles of the popular
Sèvres factory, not in contemporary taste, but tending to look
back to the 1750s: simple forms with ample surface space for
painted rural scenes often inspired by Nilson engravings.

Johann Valentin Sonnenschein, who had previously worked
at Ludwigsburg, is usually credited with modelling the
majority of the finest figures produced at Zürich between 1775–
1779. His early work at Zürich followed German models and
included musicians, peasants, soldiers and other humble
characters in contemporary costume. The larger table centrepieces (such as Bacchus astride a barrel) were probably produced towards the end of his career at the Swiss factory.

Before coming to Derby, J. J. W. Spengler spent a short
time at Zürich where he is thought to have produced about
forty different models of figures. Nearly all the moulds used at
the factory have been preserved thus making the task of the
ceramic historian comparatively easy as far as the attribution
of Zürich figures is concerned, particularly when the usual
underglaze-blue mark of a "Z" with a stroke through the
centre is not present.

Nyon

By the time hard-paste porcelain was produced at Nyon on Lake Geneva, the secret of its manufacture was widely known. In 1781 Jakob Dortu from Berlin and Ferdinand Müller of Frankenthal started a partnership which only lasted five years, after this the concern was directed by J. G. Zinkernagel until its final closure in 1813. Dortu was apparently responsible for the popular styles adopted at Nyon, often in the tedious and expensive Paris fashion of fine painting on coloured grounds, and sometimes in the simple Meissen "onion-pattern" which appears to have won universal popularity by 1780. The one outstanding decorator whose work can sometimes be identified on Nyon porcelain was Etienne Gide, a famous German miniature painter, who specialized in landscapes and figures.

The mark used on Nyon porcelain is a fish in many varying forms in underglaze-blue. This mark can easily be mistaken for the one used by the Paris decorator, Perche, in about 1825; the difference is that the decorator used the more easily applied red or brown enamel, added to the glaze by means of a stencil. There are many very good later nineteenth-century reproductions of Nyon porcelain in existence.

Hungary

The hard-paste porcelain factory established at Herend near Budapest in 1838 still produces very fine reproductions of popular eighteenth- and nineteenth-century styles of decoration, both oriental and European. The factory was started by three men who had previously been concerned with the manufacture of faience at Tata; J. G. Mayer, Vince Stingl and Móric Fischer. In 1839 the latter took over the complete enterprise employing fifty-four workers, and in order to compete with the cheaper wares made in neighbouring states, Fischer concentrated upon producing good imitations of Meissen, Sèvres or Chinese wares. These were apparently considered so good at the time that it is said that many pieces were sold in Italy as original.

Herend wares that were displayed at the 1851 Exhibition in London (such pieces as that illustrated on Pl. 9B) were much admired. Queen Victoria ordered a service decorated with flowers and butterflies for her personal use at Windsor Castle. The reproductions of Chinese enamelled wares were so convincing that Herend "replacements" were made for the original Chinese services at the Court of Turin.

When the Imperial Austrian factory at Vienna closed in 1863 Fischer was given many of the patented moulds and patterns which he used to good advantage, for at the Vienna World Exhibition of 1873 such people as the Tzar Alexander II, King Victor Emanuel and the Prince of Wales (later Edward VII), all received gifts of Herend porcelain from Emperor Francis Joseph.

Móric Fischer died in 1880. The factory, which was being run by his sons, had been declared bankrupt in 1874 but had struggled along until 1884 when it was taken over by a company of shareholders, with the state holding 30 per cent of the shares. Under this company the factory apparently made little headway and in 1896 was purchased by Jenö Farkasházy, the grandson of the founder. From this date fine quality wares were once again produced, but the intervening war years impeded progress and in 1923 the factory was formed into a company with Farkasházy remaining a director until his death in 1926. In 1948 the factory again became state owned and is today still in production as a nationalized concern.

More than ten thousand moulds of the pieces produced over the last 130 years are still in the possession of the factory and local forests still supply the fuel for the wood-burning kilns.

Unlike most modern factories, Herend does not use transfer-printed designs to give the decorators easily followed outlines: the painting is entirely free-hand, which calls for skilled painters and well-taught apprentices.

The best known Herend patterns include: The *Victoria* pattern of flowers and butterflies, *Ming*—Chinese figures in the palette of *famille rose* (Pl. 9B), *Rothschild*—birds similar to those used on Berlin wares, *Miramar*—a Chinese pink peony theme, made for the Castle Miramar of the Mexican Emperor Maximilian, *Wales*—the service made for Edward VII in which all the wares have double-walls, the outer layer being finely fretted, *Fleur des Indes*—based on the Oriental flowers of Meissen, *Sèvres Petites Roses*—in Empire style, together with all the popular Empire styles used at the Vienna factory.

Herend porcelain has always been marked but as this mark is usually in blue enamel it can of course easily be ground or etched away and a more important mark, to suggest an earlier date, added. The earliest mark was "HEREND" incised; after 1841 the initials "MF" (for Móric Fischer) appear with the year of manufacture and "HEREND". In 1848 the shield bearing the arms of Hungary was adopted together with the "MF" monogram. This monogram was replaced in 1875 by another, "F.S." From 1885 various forms of the Hungarian shield have been used together with the word "HEREND". The addition of the word "HUNGARY" denotes a date after 1891.

Early French Porcelain

Some of the most beautiful pieces of porcelain ever created

bove (Pl. 11A), plate, soft-paste porcelain in enamel colours. Mark, two 'L's enclosing 'E'. —ench (Sèvres), 1757. Diam: 9½ in.; 'cache-pot', soft-paste porcelain in enamel colours with —u céleste ground. French (Vincennes or Sèvres), *c.* 1755. Ht: 5½ in.; plate, hard-paste —rcelain in enamel colours. Mark, two 'L's under crown and 'LB' for Le Bel jeune (painter). —ench (Sèvres), *c.* 1780. Diam: 9½ in. *Below* (Pl. 11B), dish, soft-paste porcelain in enamel —ours on 'Rose Pompadour' ground. French (Sèvres), *c.* 1760. Diam: 8¾ in.; Venus and Cupid, —t-paste unglazed porcelain (biscuit). Modelled by Étienne-Maurice Falconet. French (Sèvres), 18th century. Ht: 10⅝ in.

Above (Pl. 12A), tea-caddy, hard-paste porcelain in enamel colours. Mark, 'JP' in underglaze blue. French (Fontainebleau, Jacob Petit), *c.* 1830. Ht: 7½ in.; plate, hard-paste porcelain in enamel colours. Mark, a crowned dolphin (for the Dauphin) in red. French (Lille), 1784–179[] Diam: 9 in.; cup and saucer, hard-paste porcelain in colours. Mark, 'Darte Pal. Royal No. 21' red. French (Paris, rue de la Roquette), *c.* 1830. Diam of saucer: 5½ in. *Below* (Pl. 12B), j[] hard-paste porcelain in enamel colours. Mark, 'MOL' and a star in underglaze-blue. Dut[] (Oude Loosdrecht), 1771–1784. Ht: 5⅝ in.; plate, soft-paste porcelain in enamel colours af[] Buffon. French (Tournai), 18th century. Diam: 9¾ in.; group, soft-paste porcelain in enam[] colours. French (Tournai), *c.* 1765. Ht: 8¼ in.

were of early French soft-paste porcelain. As to be expected, it was the potters already concerned with the production of tin-glazed earthenware (faience) who experimented and produced the first soft-paste porcelains in the country. By the mid-seventeenth century France was fully aware of the fine quality porcelains of the Far East and it was with such pieces in mind that the French potters made their experiments; at this date true porcelain had, of course, not yet been re-discovered in Saxony, and the only soft-paste of any consequence was the Medici porcelain produced from 1575 until about 1587 in Florence.

Some confusion still exists concerning the person responsible for the first production of soft-paste porcelain in France. Claude Révérend, a Paris potter, was granted a patent in 1664 and he claimed to "reproduce porcelain as beautiful as, or more beautiful than that which comes from the Eastern Indies". This claim would appear to be false, and no pieces of French soft-paste porcelain are known which can in any way be attributed to Révérend.

Rouen

In 1673 Louis Poterat, son of a Rouen potter, was issued with a licence to manufacture "porcelains and pottery in the fashion of Holland", but it should be noted that confusion exists over the use of the word "porcelain" which was occasionally used when "faience" was apparently intended. The pieces of porcelain attributed to Rouen by current authorities all show some relationship to the contemporary gold and silver shapes and the more common Rouen faience. The porcelain body has a bluish or greenish tinge, the glaze is usually clear and wet-looking, and the underglaze-blue decoration, dark and inky. Cups usually follow the Chinese tea-bowl fashion and have no handles. Almost all the porcelains attributed to Rouen are decorated in the same manner as the faience; that is with *lambrequins* or loop decoration. Unless more definite information comes to light, the porcelains attributed to Rouen will always be regarded with some doubt.

Saint-Cloud

The collector is on much more certain ground when identifying the soft-paste produced at Saint-Cloud near Paris, from about 1690 until the factory ceased in 1766. In 1702 Louis XIV granted letters patent to the widow of Pierre Chicaneau who had died in 1678. The process of manufacturing soft-paste porcelain had apparently been discovered by her husband prior to his death and his widow and family had improved upon the process until in 1693 they were claiming to produce wares equal to those of the Far East. Following upon the death of her husband, Chicaneau's widow married another potter, Henri Trou, whose son appears to have taken a great interest in the factory. A rival factory was set up near Paris by a member of the Chicaneau-Trou family in 1722; this continued until 1742, when the two concerns united.

The early soft-paste of Saint-Cloud is often similar to that of the Chelsea factory. Their wares were seldom large, which suggests that warping was a great problem, and this is further borne out by the comparatively thick potting of all Saint-Cloud wares. This factory was probably the first to introduce the *trembleuse*, the saucer with the raised ring to prevent the cup slipping, as illustrated in Pl. 10A. This photograph also shows the typically square-sectioned handle which was used so often at Saint-Cloud, as well as the popular relief scaling in the form of an artichoke. Other popular shapes were the typical upright cylinder with a slightly domed lid (as also used at Mennecy: Pl. 10A) and the three-lobed spicebox, whose lid could be twirled aside to reveal the three compartments.

Saint-Cloud porcelain particularly lent itself to the imitation of Chinese *blanc-de-Chine* porcelain which was brought to

Europe in large quantities from the late seventeenth century onwards; the most popular of these copies show the prunus sprigs applied in relief. Rouen faience again set the fashion of *lambrequins, style rayonnant* and similar grotesque and scroll-like ornament in underglaze-blue.

Precise dating of Saint-Cloud wares is difficult. The early wares appear rather whiter than the later creamy-toned pieces, but it is sometimes possible to arrive at a more definite date when a piece has a hall-marked silver mount.

Saint-Cloud produced some beautifully modelled snuff-boxes in the form of various animals, the mounts of which often bear dates between 1730 and 1750, as well as similarly well modelled cane-handles in human forms. These small objects are often decorated in both the style and palette of the Japanese Kakiemon porcelain. The larger porcelain figures are rather rare and, according to an advertisement of 1731, are among the later productions of the Saint-Cloud factory. The Chinaman on Pl. 10B is an outstanding example and similarly sparingly painted in the Japanese Kakiemon palette.

The majority of Saint-Cloud practical wares are marked. The early mark on the white porcelain taking the form of a sun-face which is always in underglaze-blue, while the later, and more common mark, is "S^{t}C" over "T" (Saint-Cloud/ Trou) and is applied either in blue or by incising into the clay.

Chantilly

The second famous soft-paste porcelain factory of France was not established until 1725. The proprietor, Ciquaire Cirou, enjoyed the patronage of Louis-Henri de Bourbon, Prince de Condé, until the time of his death in 1740. The Prince was a great lover of Japanese porcelain and probably used his influence to persuade the King to grant Cirou a twenty-year patent to produce porcelain in imitation of the Japanese. Cirou himself died in 1751, and after this the factory was run by a succession of unimportant proprietors until about 1800.

The finest porcelain of Chantilly was made from 1725 until about 1740 when the Prince died. His collection of Japanese porcelain was undoubtedly used by the factory when they were making the fine reproductions of the Far Eastern wares. The palette of Kakiemon would obviously have looked wrong on the creamy soft-paste body of the normal Chantilly ware. To remedy this they prepared a more suitable ground by rendering the usual clear glaze, opaque with tin-oxide. Thus upon this white ground, more akin to the original Japanese porcelain, the painters were able to apply their colours in the style of their patron's original pieces. One cannot accuse the modellers of only copying Japanese wares, for many other shapes, after Meissen or contemporary silver, were also introduced.

These original styles were abandoned in the middle of the eighteenth century and the opaque-glaze was replaced by a clear glaze as the wares of Chantilly came under the influence of Vincennes; the factory which had been started up in 1738 with the aid of Chantilly workmen. Japanese painting was replaced by the naturalistic flowers made popular at Meissen but now taking on a more mellow look with the colours being partially absorbed by the soft glaze.

During the second half of the century the currently popular "Chantilly sprig" was introduced and many plates were painted in either underglaze-blue or enamel blue with this much copied form decorating the entire ground with sketchily painted flowers (Pl. 10A). Another popular underglaze-blue decoration consists of a garden-fountain beneath an arched trellis; many plates decorated in this manner also have the borders of the *osier* (basketwork) pattern, which was introduced at Meissen.

The recognized mark of Chantilly is the French hunting-horn in red enamel. This is most usually seen on the wares with the opacified glaze, later the mark is normally underglaze-blue, or indeed any convenient enamel colour which the painter happened to have to hand. Sometimes the name "Chantilly" is painted in full, though on occasions the name of the Château, (such as "Villers cotteret") occurs.

The original factory closed down in about 1800, but other factories of little importance continued into the nineteenth century producing hard-paste porcelain copies of the eighteenth-century styles. One such factory, set up by Pigory the Mayor of Chantilly, used the hunting-horn mark, together with "P". Another such factory produced wares with "M.A." for the owner Michael Aaron.

Mennecy

Among the finest of all soft-paste porcelains are the wares and figures produced at Mennecy. This factory was first established in 1734 by François Barbin who was protected by Louis-François de Neufville, duc de Villeroy. Between 1734 and 1748 the factory was situated in the rue de Charonne; it was then transferred to Mennecy where it remained until 1773, when it was moved once again to Bourg-la-Reine, until it eventually closed in 1806. During the final twenty years it is probable that only cream-coloured earthenware was produced.

The beauty of the early Mennecy porcelain is that it is so obviously a soft-paste. The paste is a milky-white, the glaze "wet" and brilliant, absorbing the well-known Mennecy rose-pink enamel until it almost appears to run. Because of the harsh monopolies of the Vincennes-Sèvres factory, Mennecy was prohibited from using gilding, so that the same rose-pink or bright blue was used to paint the edges of the table-wares.

The shapes of Mennecy were few and simple, providing ample space for their own versions of the *Deutsche Blumen* of Meissen (Pl. 10A). Most of the practical wares were small and included some delightful covered custard-cups with close spiral reeding and miniature urns fashioned after garden ornaments.

One of the many mistakes for which an amateur collector may be forgiven would be to confuse some of the figures of Mennecy with those of the English Bow factory. These figures were made about 1760, apparently to sit in the centre of a table; the groups are composed of children, obviously inspired by Boucher (Pl. 10B). Of equal beauty, but more difficult to identify with certainty, are the white glazed figures such as a River God, a Naiad, and Diana.

Mennecy, in common with Chantilly, made many small items such as snuff-boxes, scent-bottles and knife-handles. These wares were rarely marked and it is well to bear in mind the colours of rose-pink, bright blue, and brownish-green as being peculiar to the Mennecy factory.

The most common mark on Mennecy porcelain is "D.V." for "de Villeroy"; occasionally seen in red or blue enamel, it is usually in the more readily acceptable form of being incised into the clay before firing. In 1765 the factory was purchased by Joseph Jullien and Symphorien Jacques, who ran the factory together with that of Sceaux, which they had purchased in 1762. In 1772 they sold Sceaux and a year later transferred their Mennecy production to a new works at Bourg-la-Reine, and in consequence adopted the mark "BR".

Vincennes and Sèvres

Amateur collectors will do well to remember that there are probably more pieces of porcelain which have been deliberately decorated and falsely marked so that they appear to be genuine early Vincennes or Sèvres, than of any other type of faked porcelain.

This important French factory was first started in 1738, when Orry de Fulvy obtained the services of Gilles and Robert Dubois. These Chantilly workmen claimed they knew how to produce porcelain, but in 1741, after having spent a great deal of money, their claims proved false and they were dismissed. Their successor, François Gravant, who also came from Chantilly, was more successful and in 1745 a company was formed under the name of Charles Adam, and Orry de Fulvy was replaced by Jean-Baptiste Machault, a very competent organizer and a patron of the arts. The first privilege was granted to Vincennes at this time to make porcelain "in the Saxon fashion (i.e. painted and gilded) with human figures". Factories throughout France were prohibited from making similar wares, the workmen were barred from seeking employment elsewhere, and in any case other factories were forbidden to engage any men who dared to leave the factory. A similar, even harsher order was issued in 1747 concerning the behaviour of the workers to ensure the secrets of the methods of production did not leak to other factories. In 1753 further privileges were granted to the new Eloi Brichard concern, which replaced the Charles Adam company; one privilege tried to prohibit other factories from even adding decoration to earthenware (faience). King Louis XV was now deeply interested in this new venture and contributed a quarter of the necessary capital.

It was decided in 1753 to transfer the factory from the royal château at Vincennes to a more convenient site at Sèvres, between Paris and Vincennes, close to the château of Madame de Pompadour at Bellevue. This new building, which was later criticized as being entirely unsuitable as a factory, was completed and occupied in 1756. Despite new premises, the wares produced were obviously too costly, for by 1759 the factory was so much in debt that the creditors proposed closure; prompted by the administrative director Boileau, the King himself purchased the factory.

After Machault's appointment in 1745, various court artists, craftsmen and sculptors were requested to direct their skills towards making beautiful porcelain. Jean Hellot, the chemist, was responsible for many of the unsurpassed ground-colours, Duplessis, the royal goldsmith, for designs, Mathieu, the enameller, for modelling and decoration, while Hulst (or Hults) acted as general adviser upon styles. The process of the superb gilding of early Sèvres was purchased from Frère Hippolyte, a Benedictine monk, who was paid a large annuity. The authenticity of a piece of Sèvres can quite often be judged purely on the quality of the gilding alone.

Although it was originally intended that Sèvres should produce hard-paste porcelain "in the style of the Saxon" (meaning Meissen), only the more beautiful soft-paste porcelain was produced until the discovery of the essential clays at Saint-Yrieix, near Limoges. These clay deposits were purchased by Louis XV in 1769 for use in his factory. The wares which were produced in the new hard-paste were called *Porcelaine Royale* to distinguish them from the earlier soft-paste or *Porcelaine de France* (Pl. 11A). Hard-paste wares were not made in any quantity until 1772, and from this time the manufacture of hard-paste gradually took the place of the soft-paste until in about 1804, the production of soft-paste (*pâté tendre*) was finally abandoned as being too costly.

The wares produced at Vincennes until 1753 are sometimes difficult to attribute correctly, for although the royal cypher of the crossed "L's" was sometimes used, it was not until 1753 that the device was declared to be the factory-mark and date-letters were added; such as A for 1753, B for 1754 and so on until the final PP, which marks the end of the royal period in 1793.

The output between 1745–48 was apparently much in the style of the earlier Chantilly factory, where so many wares had been made in the Japanese styles featuring the designs and palette of the so-called "Kakiemon". Use was also made of the naturalistic flowers of Meissen, which acquired a new charm on the soft-paste body, and scenes such as those associated with the German painter Herold also appeared, though in less ornate Baroque surrounds.

By 1750 the almost perfect soft-paste was being produced in the graceful French shapes of the period; jugs with long cylindrical necks, ice-pails and slender vases with trumpet-shaped mouths. These wares were decorated with a French interpretation of the Meissen flowers, taking on a rather un-natural and stylized arrangement. Monochrome painting in either crimson or blue enamel was also used, the latter often having the addition of the flesh-tints to the figures, a style of decoration attributed to Vieillard (1752–90). At times only the exquisite gilding was employed or it was occasionally coupled with the famous underglaze-blue ground (*gros bleu*), a colour introduced in 1749.

The years in which the various ground colours were intro-duced should be remembered in order to check with the year mark, as certain colours cannot pre-date certain years. The underglaze-blue, with its variation in depth of colour (*gros bleu*) was the first of these colours and was introduced in 1749; the popular turquoise (*bleu céleste*) (Pl. 11A), as was so often reproduced in nineteenth-century wares, in 1752; yellow or *jaune jonquille* in 1753; pea-green in 1756, and the powdery pink, *rose Pompadour* in 1757 (Pl. 11B); traditionally this last colour is said to have not been used after the death of Madame de Pompadour in 1764. The term '*rose du Barry*' is simply an English alternative for *rose Pompadour*.

The most beautiful porcelain ever produced at Vincennes probably includes the bowls, teapots and cups and saucers in '*gros bleu*' with gilt birds painted by Mutel in reserved panels. Figures and birds in landscapes were also painted by such artists as Aloncle, Xhrouet, Gomery and many others, all leaving the white porcelain as a background in their painting. All too soon the painters tended to fill in the entire reserve panel, lending a heavy appearance that should not be associated with soft-paste. After 1753 the painters and gilders were permitted to identify their work with their initials or a device; these, together with the known dates of their employment in the factory are all recorded, as well as the type of decoration in which they specialized. This combined information often helps to detect a forgery more easily. For instance, no hard-paste porcelain should bear a date-letter prior to "P" (for 1768) at the very earliest, "T" (for 1772) being more acceptable. No ground colour should have a date-letter pre-dating its introduction; thus "E" (for 1757) should be the earliest mark seen on *rose Pompadour*. Then the painters and gilders: were they active during the year suggested by the date letter, and are they known to have painted in the manner of the piece in question? For example, Bardet painted flowers between 1751–58, Chabry, pastorals 1765–87, Dodin, figures 1754–1802, and Evans, birds 1752–1806. Armed with all these facts, (which are readily available in mark-books) even the amateur can often feel quite confident in condemning a piece as a forgery.

Many early Meissen porcelain figures appear to have found their way to France. These pieces are sometimes seen on very fine ormolu mounts, often with a metal bocage with stems terminating in beautifully made soft-paste porcelain flowers. Such porcelain blooms were apparently in great demand, for according to the early Vincennes factory records five-sixths of the total output in 1749 was of such flowers. It is also recorded

that Madame de Pompadour received the King in a con-
servatory decorated with masses of porcelain flowers, all
perfumed accordingly.

The Dauphine Marie-Josèphe was apparently so eager to
show her father, the Elector of Saxony, the beauty of French
porcelain that she arranged to send him a bouquet composed
of four hundred and eighty porcelain flowers. Because of their
fragile nature they were carried in a wheel-barrow for the
entire journey. They obviously arrived safely for the flowers
(in a white vase) are still in the State Porcelain Collection at
Dresden.

The people responsible for the assembly and sale of the
extravagant French ornaments were known as *marchands-
merciers*. These same middle-men were instrumental in
compiling the individual work of the finest furniture and
bronze makers, and so creating the wonderful court furniture
of the period. The early Vincennes porcelain figures were
often mounted in fine ormolu in this same manner.

According to Jean-Jacques Bachelier, who was Art-Director
at Vincennes and Sèvres from 1751–93, the earliest figures of
Vincennes were coloured; but such pieces are either rarely
seen or remain unidentified. The early glazed figures (left
white) are of beautiful soft-paste porcelain and feature such
characters as River Gods, Naiads, Diana, and children
modelled after Boucher. These early models were created by
such people as Goubet, Laurent, Blondeau, Bulidon and
Herbert, and were original work expressly produced for reproduction in porcelain. The biscuit porcelain groups which
were to prove so popular were not produced until about 1750
and merited mention in the sales lists of Lazare Duvaux, the
well-known *marchand-mercier*, in 1753. Glazed figures were
still made after this date but are definitely less common.

The man whose name is particularly associated with Sèvres
biscuit porcelain was Etienne Maurice Falconet who was in

charge of the modelling between 1757 and 1766. Falconet had modelled for the factory since about 1755, but much of his early work obviously came under the influence of Boucher, especially the groups depicting children (Pl. 11B). From 1757 his work is far more original and such pieces as "*Pygmalion*" and the "*Baigneuse*" (the Bather) remained so popular that they merited many later nineteenth-century reproductions.

In 1766 Falconet left for Russia at the invitation of Catherine II, and from this date the Sèvres factory relied mainly upon reduced versions of the work of such established sculptors as Pigalle, Bouchardon, Clodion, Houdon and Saly. Louis-Simon Boizot was placed in charge of the modelling department in 1774. The majority of his models were produced in the new hard-paste porcelain and included such monumental assemblies as the coronation group of Louis XVI and Marie Antoinette. In 1780 Boizot was succeeded by his chief assistant, Le Riche, who remained head of the modelling department until 1801. From about 1782 production included many busts and statues of famous men: reduced versions of famous bronzes or marbles, but the hard-paste material was entirely unsuitable for reproducing the effect of marble, and in many cases tends to look more like plaster of paris.

One of the greatest aids to the recognition of true Sèvres porcelain is the superb quality of the gilding which was usually applied thickly, revealing fine chasing upon close examination (Pl. 11A). This gilding is seen at its best on the beautiful underglaze-blue ground. Unfortunately this colour was superseded in about 1760 by the all too perfect enamel colour of *bleu de roi*. This "Royal" blue is the colour so often seen on both Continental and English copies of Sèvres. The English factory of Coalport made some very fine examples of "Sèvres-type" wares using the *bleu de roi* ground.

The French decorators introduced some novel and effective methods of subduing many of the later and rather vivid colour-grounds by overpainting the entire ground-colour with such devices as the "*oeil-de-perdrix*" (partridge-eye), small gilt spotted rings surrounding a white circle, "*caillouté*" (pebbled), pebble-shaped gilt lines drawn as an irregular mesh, and "*vermiculé*", the breaking up of the entire ground with "rivers" of gilding or enamel colour, and scale-patterns.

A type of decoration which appears a great deal on later reproductions of Sèvres is the so-called "jewelled" decoration. This is most effective when used in a restrained manner and consists of drops of suitably coloured enamels fused over gilt or silver foil to imitate rubies, emeralds and turquoise. This method is said to have been introduced by Cotteau during the time he was at Sèvres (1780–84), which means that any piece decorated in this manner and bearing a date-letter prior to "CC" is almost certainly a nineteenth-century reproduction or an early piece of porcelain decorated at a later date.

The authorities of the Sèvres factory rather encouraged the nineteenth-century forgers of earlier wares, for in 1793, 1800, 1804 and 1813 large quantities of slightly faulty or undecorated soft-paste porcelain, made during the "Royal period", were sold off. These wares were then re-decorated by such people as R. Robins and T. M. Randall in England and Soiron in Paris; the latter had actually worked at the Sèvres factory. Soft-paste porcelain which has had decoration added at a later date can often be recognized by the presence of minute "black-heading" on the surface of the glaze, particularly noticeable within the foot-rims of bowls, cups and saucers or dishes. These nineteenth-century forgers could rarely resist the urge to mark their pieces with the early date-letters of A, B or C, consequently often pre-dating the style of their decoration. Similarly, before the nineteenth century, no pieces are known to have been made bearing portraits of the Royal family or notable Court personages.

Samson of Paris made many copies of biscuit figures in the

Falconet style, but his form of mark (as illustrated at the Chapter heading) is usually quite distinct.

After 1792 the factory of Sèvres ceased to function as a royal factory, and the wares produced during the first few years of the Republic have little to interest collectors. In 1800 Napoleon Bonaparte placed Alexandre Brongniart in charge of the factory. Brongniart's first decision was to abandon the production of the costly soft-paste and produce only true porcelain.

The majority of the wares made at Sèvres during the early nineteenth century appear overdecorated to our eyes, and often employed newly introduced ground-colours, sometimes imitating tortoiseshell or wood. Many large services and vases were made in the popular Empire or Egyptian styles. After the death of Brongniart in 1847 the manufacture of soft-paste was resumed for a short while by his successor Ebelman.

Credit is given to Riocreux (Curator of the Musée Céramique at Sèvres) for the introduction of *pâte-sur-pâte*, the application of white porcelain paste to a coloured ground to achieve a cameo-like effect. This style of decoration is particularly associated with Marc-Louis Solon who later worked at the Minton factory.

Paris and other French hard-paste Porcelain Factories

Although the soft-paste porcelains of France are considered their finest wares by collectors today, the aim of the majority of French factories was undoubtedly to produce wares in the less expensive hard-paste porcelain. There were, however, certain factories such as Saint-Amand, where the production of soft-paste continued until the late nineteenth century.

The first hard-paste porcelain to be produced in France was made at the factory of Charles-François Hannong at Strasbourg by his son Paul, who probably used clays imported from Germany. After disagreements with the management of Vincennes, Hannong moved to Frankenthal where he produced hard-paste porcelain under the protection of the Elector Palatine in 1755.

From about 1770 onwards numerous hard-paste porcelain factories were set up in Paris which were often able to operate in defiance of the various privileges enjoyed by Sèvres because they too were protected by members of the Royal family.

There is little to choose between the various factories in either quality or style and if it were not that distinctive marks were invariably used, identification would be almost impossible. The four outstanding Paris factories enjoying such protection were:

Clignacourt
Founded in 1771 by Deruelle, the hard-paste porcelain factory of Clignacourt was protected by Monsieur le Comte de Provence, brother of Louis XVI, who succeeded in time, becoming Louis XVIII (1814–24). The practical porcelain wares were of a fine quality and the decoration sometimes signed by the painter George Lamprecht who specialized in the painting of figures and animals at Sèvres (1784–87). The various marks used at Clignacourt include a windmill in either underglaze-blue or gold, the monogram of Louis-Stanislas-Xavier (*Monsieur*) stencilled in red or a crowned "M". The factory closed in about 1798.

Rue Thiroux
Porcelain made at the rue Thiroux was known as "*porcelaine*

de la reine" since the factory had been protected by Queen Marie Antoinette from the time of its establishment by Leboeuf in 1775. Despite the execution of its patron this factory continued under various owners until about 1870. The productions of rue Thiroux conformed to the usual Parisian taste in high quality porcelains. The easily recognized mark was a crowned "A" in underglaze-blue or the letter "A" stencilled in red enamel.

Rue de Bondy

The factory of rue de Bondy was established in 1780 by Dihl under the patronage of the Duc d'Angoulême (after whom the well-known "Angoulême sprig" was named). Dihl is best known for his partnership with Guerhard, which started in 1786; the partnership continued with Dihl's widow until 1817. The name of the protector consequently is a constant reminder of the type of decoration seen on a great deal of the porcelain produced by this factory; the popular sprig pattern of such flowers as the cornflower, but this pattern also appears on the wares of other late French factories and several English concerns. Several different marks were used during the lifetime of the factory, the earliest being forms of "A.G." (Angoulême-Guerhard) with or without a crown in gold or underglaze-blue, "*MANUFRE de Mon le Duc d'Angoulême*", or "*MANUFRE de MM Guerhard et Dihl à Paris*", stencilled in red, or "Dihl" in red or underglaze-blue.

Faubourg Saint-Denis

The factory of Faubourg Saint-Denis was first established by Pierre-Antoine Hannong in 1771 and, as a result of the protection of Charles-Philippe, Comte d'Artois, made wares of a type not normally permitted outside Sèvres. This factory continued to flourish after the Revolution, especially during the time of the last proprietor, Marc Schoelcher, who continued until 1828. The common marks were crossed "smoking-pipes", in underglaze-blue, "CP" under a crown (Charles-Philippe) in red, blue or gold, or the name Schoelcher.

Apart from these most important factories the following also produced large quantities of similar wares:

La Courtille

A further highly productive Paris porcelain factory was established at La Courtille in the rue Fontaine-au-Roy in 1771 by Jean-Baptiste Locré de Roissy. Although under the management of a German modeller, Laurentius Russinger, the fine quality wares were decorated in the current Parisian styles but the mark of two crossed torches in underglaze-blue or incised was obviously intended to imitate the crossed-swords of Meissen. Porcelain from La Courtille was obviously exported as several pieces are known to have been painted by William Billingsley, the Derby painter who eventually set up his own factory at Nantgarw in South Wales. In addition to practical wares, particularly well modelled biscuit porcelain figures were produced at La Courtille under the direction of Russinger. In 1800 he took a Limoges potter named Pouyat into partnership, the factory continuing under the proprietorship of Pouyat and his family until finally closing in 1840.

Rue de la Roquette

Another factory, whose mark of crossed arrows can sometimes be confused with Meissen, was established by Vincent Dubois in the rue de la Roquette in 1774, continuing until about 1787. This factory produced little porcelain worthy of mention. In the first quarter of the nineteenth century a further factory was set up by Darte *frères*, established about 1795 in rue de Charonne, later moving to rue de la Roquette and rue Popincourt (Pl. 12A). They also had a decorating establishment in the

Palais Royal which accounts for the marks "DARTE/-FRERES/A PARIS" and "DARTE/Pal. Royal/No. 21", stencilled in red.

Lille

The plate illustrated in Pl. 12A was made at a French hard-paste porcelain factory started in 1784 by Leperre-Durot under the protection of the Dauphin. This factory is of particular interest as it was apparently one of the first to fire its kilns with coal. Once again wares were styled and decorated in the popular Parisian styles, but there was obviously a demand for such pieces as the factory continued under various proprietors until 1817. The amusing mark is a rather badly stencilled little fish in red, which is at times difficult to recognize as such.

Limoges

The existence of the two essential ingredients of hard-paste porcelain, china-clay and china-stone, at Saint Yrieix near Limoges was known as early as 1764, but it was not until 1768 that the Royal factory of Sèvres made use of these deposits. Limoges became the centre of the French ceramic industry, and since the nineteenth century numerous factories engaged in the manufacture of hard-paste porcelain of a very dull type have sprung up. The first Limoges hard-paste porcelain factory was established in 1771 by the two brothers Grellet under the protection of the Comte d'Artois. In 1784 the factory was taken over by the King to produce hard-paste porcelain which was decorated at Sèvres. The factory ceased production in 1796. The mark most often used was "CD" (Comte d'Artois) incised, and in red, crimson or underglaze-blue, with the occasional addition of the Sèvres mark and painter. A rarer mark is a *fleur-de-lis* impressed or incised.

The initials of the proprietor often accompany the word Limoges, while the word "FRANCE" indicates a date after

1891. The marks most frequently seen are: "CA" monogram (Charles Ahrenfeldt, 1894-); "B. & Cie" (Belleroy); "J. B. & Cie" (Julien Balleroy & Cie); "B. & Co". (Bernardaud & Cie, 1863-); "BRP" (Beulé, Reboisson & Parot); "C. F. & P." (Chaufriasse, Rougérie & Co.); "F.M." (Fontanille & Marraud, 1925-).

Fontainebleau

There are a certain number of French hard-paste porcelain wares decorated in the extravagant revived-Rococo style which have much in common with some Rockingham. It is essential therefore to carefully check whether the body is the Continental hard-paste or the English bone-china. Many of these French pieces are the work of Jacob and Mardochée Petit, who took over in 1830 an earlier factory established in 1795 by Benjamin Jacob and Aaron Smoll at Fontainebleau. They are sometimes marked "J.P." in underglaze-blue or incised (Pl. 12A).

Niderviller

The hard-paste porcelain factory at Niderviller has a long history; commencing in 1765, it continues in production to the present day. It was originally founded in 1754 by Baron Jean-Louis de Bayerlé for the production of faience but from 1765, small quantities of hard-paste porcelain were also produced. In 1770 the concern was purchased by the Comte de Custine, but on his death it went to Claude-François Lanfrey.

The factory was obviously very much influenced by the Strasbourg factory of the Hannongs (of which it was an off-shoot), as its styles show the same German Rococo taste in their imposing vases, clocks and large table-wares. Furthermore, there is really very little difference between the forms and decorations of the factory's faience and porcelains, the same Oriental or European flowers, sprigs or landscapes being used on both bodies.

The majority of Niderviller hard-paste porcelain figures were left in the biscuit state; in many cases they were modelled by Charles Sauvage, also known as Lemire. Other models are often the work of Cyfflé, who had his own factory at Lunéville between 1766 and 1777. When this was sold in 1780, many of his moulds passed to Niderviller. The marks on Niderviller porcelain were, "BN" in monogram for "Beyerlé", "CN" monogram or two interlaced "C's" (Custine) or "N", "Nider", or "Niderviller" in full.

Holland

Holland's porcelain is not so well known as its earlier Delftware, nor is much sought after by collectors. This is probably due to the fact that rarely was anything produced in any of the Dutch porcelain factories which was entirely original in either shape or decoration. The fact that Holland, through the trading of the Dutch East India Company (founded 1609), was probably better acquainted with Chinese porcelain than most other European countries seems to have made very little difference to the porcelains of such factories as Weesp, Oude Loosdrecht, Amstel and The Hague.

Weesp

Unlike the majority of German factories, the factory established in 1759 at Weesp was an entirely commercial concern and enjoyed no privileges. An Irishman named Daniel MacCarthy had established an earthenware factory in 1757, but this apparently failed and two years later the same factory was taken over by Count van Gronsveldt-Diepenbroik.

Porcelain was probably not produced in any quantity before 1762.

Van Gronsveldt, who had been Dutch Ambassador in Berlin, appears to have had early access to knowledge relating to the production of hard-paste porcelain, but it was probably Nikolaus Paul, the arcanist of Wegely's Berlin factory, who was responsible for the short-lived success of Weesp porcelain.

The china-stone used at Weesp was obtained from Germany and produced fine white wares of a high technical quality and, although the style of decoration was similar to the current German fashions, the majority of the decorators appear to have come from France. At one time the factory of Sèvres was interested in taking over the Dutch concern, obviously with a view to making hard-paste porcelain, for at the time (1767) only soft-paste was being produced at the Royal factory. The painting was generally of a high quality and consisted of "Watteau-like" figures in landscapes, naturalistic flowers or exotic birds, the latter being painted in rather exaggeratedly bright colours.

Very few figures can be attributed to Weesp, but those known are of such pastoral characters as nymphs and shepherds with the necessary cupids. Most of these simply have a white glaze finish. The only modeller whose name can be safely associated with these figures is Nicolas-François Gauron who had previously worked at Mennecy, Vincennes, and Tournai.

The mark employed by Weesp was a blatant copy of the Meissen crossed-swords in underglaze-blue with the addition of three dots between the points of the blades and on either side.

In 1771 the factory was purchased by Johannes de Mol, a pastor, who transferred the factory to Oude Loosdrecht, near Hilversum.

Oude Loosdrecht

The moulds of the Weesp factory were put to use at the commencement of the Oude Loosdrecht factory (in about 1774). But it soon followed the common tendency to abandon German styles for those being made universally popular at Sèvres in the so-called *Louis Seize* style, the transitional style between Rococo and Neo-classical. The majority of the well-proportioned table-wares were produced with ample plain surfaces which allowed the decorators more latitude than had been possible on styles of Weesp. Landscapes were especially popular, (Pl. 12B) in either the full enamel palette or brown, black or purple monochrome. The few figure subjects produced at Oude Loosdrecht consisted almost entirely of biscuit-busts of popular historical figures on biscuit or glazed pedestals.

The mark used at Loosdrecht until it failed in 1784 was "M.O.L." either incised, or in underglaze-blue, black or coloured enamels. These initials could stand for either "*Manufactuur Oude Loosdrecht*" or the name of Johannes de Mol (*d.* 1782). (Mol. Oude Loosdrecht).

Amstel

In 1784 this concern was again transferred, this time from Oude Loosdrecht to Ouder Amstel near Amsterdam where good quality porcelain was made under the direction of Friedrich Däuber, another German. The wares produced at Amstel followed, almost without deviation, the forms and styles of decoration previously employed at Loosdrecht; quality of the highest but lacking any new ideas, although towards 1800 the designs were obviously very much under the influence of the popular Parisian porcelain manufacturers who were then producing table-wares in the Empire style. When Däuber died in 1800, the factory came up for auction and was purchased by G. Dommer & Co., who in 1809 removed the concern once again to Nieuwer Amstel, where production continued in almost identical styles until 1820.

Sometimes the mark of "M.O.L." (as above) is to be seen together with the word Amstel, suggesting that certain wares made at Oude Loosdrecht were decorated after the factory had been transferred to Amstel. At other times the word "Amstel" is written in black.

The Hague

It was yet another German who was responsible for porcelain manufacture at The Hague. Anton Lyncker, who probably came from Saxony, was first concerned with Saxon and Thuringian porcelain which he imported into Holland in "the white" and then decorated it. This accounts for the marks of such factories as Tournai, Ansbach, Höchst and Meissen being accompanied by the overglaze-blue mark of The Hague stork with an eel in its beak. Although Lyncker was first recorded as a dealer in 1773 it was not until about 1776 that he actually started to manufacture hard-paste porcelain. His factory apparently flourished and he exported a large amount of his wares to the Near East. Although Lyncker died in 1781 the factory continued in production under his widow and son for a further nine years.

As is the case with other Dutch porcelain factories, few wares were made which show originality. The tea-services, which they seem to have specialized in, were again in the practical Neo-classical styles, occasionally decorated by Leonardus Temminck, one of their better-known painters whose speciality was Boucher-like cupids in purple monochrome, similar to those of Richard Askew, the Derby painter.

The only mark which can be regarded as indicating both porcelain and decoration of The Hague is of course that depicting the stork with the eel in its beak in underglaze-blue. This device is the emblem of the city.

Belgium

Tournai

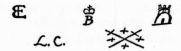

The soft-paste porcelain produced at Tournai between 1750 and about 1800 has always attracted the attention of collectors but is often difficult to identify when unmarked. François Joseph Peterinck was granted a patent in 1751 by the Empress Maria Theresa and the factory remained under his direction until just prior to his death in 1799, at the age of eighty.

The fact that many English potters and decorators were employed by Peterinck during the 1760s undoubtedly accounts for the similarity of much Tournai porcelain with the wares of Derby and Worcester. W. B. Honey suggests that workers from Tournai might well have played a part in the creation of the Chelsea "gold-anchor" styles.

At first the porcelain of Tournai had a slightly grey hue, but from about 1765 onwards it appears in the usual accepted creaminess of soft-pastes. The styles of Meissen and Sèvres were of course copied. The basketwork (*osier*) borders of the Saxon factory were particularly popular and are sometimes seen together with a more original spirally curved ribbing; while Rococo styles are apparent on the large table-wares the approach is restrained and reduced to simple scrolls.

The early styles of decoration copied from Meissen include typical naturalistic flowers in a paler palette in keeping with the body of soft-paste, and the well-known "onion-pattern" which became a little too blurred under the soft-glaze; the flower-sprays with occasional gilt outlines look far happier.

Henri-Joseph Duvivier is credited with almost all the finest painting on Tournai porcelain. He was the chief painter at the factory from 1763–71 and to his hand is attributed the painting of the exotic birds and figures. His palette shows a preference for a warm red-brown in landscapes and a pleasing crimson monochrome to depict Sèvres-type cupids or Meissen-type scenes of castles, with equestrian figures. Perhaps the best known service produced at Tournai is that illustrated on Pl. 12B. This is said to have been made for the Duke of Orleans in 1787; the bird painting is after the illustrations in Buffon's *Histoire Naturelle des Oiseaux* published in 1786.

The blue enamel ground (*bleu de roi*) appears on many Tournai pieces, and the Buffon birds were obviously very popular, as many other pieces, not from the service of the Duke, were decorated in the same style. The artist responsible for this bird-painting was Jean-Ghislain-Joseph Mayer who became head painter at the factory in 1774.

Tournai apparently supplied a large amount of undecorated porcelain to The Hague, and any soft-paste piece marked with the enamel Hague mark of a stork is almost certainly to have come from the Belgian factory.

A new collector may be somewhat comforted by the knowledge that even highly experienced collectors sometimes have difficulty in deciding whether a figure is Derby or Tournai, as these factories often left their figures unmarked. The chief sculptor at Tournai from 1758–64 was Nicolas-Joseph Gauron who had previously been at Mennecy and was later to go to Weesp, Chelsea and Derby. Joseph Willems, the sculptor from the Chelsea factory, was probably responsible for introducing many English styles to Tournai. Willems was born at Brussels and returned to Tournai in 1766, but died within the year.

In *English Porcelain Figures of the 18th century* (Faber), Arthur Lane has reprinted the inventory of Willem's models as originally listed by Soil de Moriamé, the first historian of Tournai. Many of the listed groups and figures were related to the Chelsea factory and provided ideal models for the Tournai modellers.

The majority of the models produced after the death of Willems have been attributed to Antoine Gillis and Nicolas Lecreux. The groups are usually left in the white glazed finish, but when painted in enamel as in Pl. 12B, the rather strong colours are a distinctive feature. The composition of the "Bird-Nesters" (Pl. 12B), a group around a tree, is indicative of the work of Lecreux, as also are the rock-like bases with applied flowers.

After his death in 1797, the factory was continued by Peterinck's son until 1800 when he left to establish a new earthenware factory which continued until 1885 in the same town. The original factory was taken over by J.-M.-J. de Bettignies, a son-in-law of the founder, and continued until it was taken over by Boch *frères* in 1850. It was during the Bettignies period that so many of the blatant forgeries of Sèvres, Chelsea and Worcester were produced both at Tournai and their other factory at Saint-Amand-les-Eaux.

The early Tournai wares were marked with a tower (from the arms of Tournai) either in coloured enamels or gold, but from about 1760 this mark appears to have been reserved for their finer wares. The more common mark of two crossed-swords having crosses in the four angles was applied in blue on nearly all other wares from about 1756–81. Many of the later fine wares, such as the "Buffon-service", were left unmarked. There is a late form of forgery made in Tournai itself complete with a rather oversize tower mark.

In her *Journals*, Lady Charlotte Schrieber describes how, in 1877, she witnessed the production of forgeries in such soft-paste porcelains as those made at Sèvres, Saint-Cloud, Chantilly, Sceaux, Chelsea and Worcester, all being made by the Bettignies.

Brussels

There were three minor porcelain factories at Brussels which warrant attention. The first was in existence from 1786–90 at Schaerbeck, near Brussels; the proprietor was J.-S. Vaume. Its productions, which show no originality, merely copying the popular Paris styles, are marked with a "B", with or without a crown, in red enamel.

In 1787 Chrétien Kuhne established a further hard-paste porcelain factory at Etterbeek which survived until 1803. In addition to the usual French-style table-wares he is known to have produced figures in both biscuit and glazed porcelain. His mark was "EB" in monogram in red or purple.

There is some doubt as to whether the factory of Louis Cretté which was established in about 1791, actually produced porcelain or merely decorated wares from other factories. He is certainly known to have sometimes decorated La Courtille porcelain, and wares marked "L. Cretté Bruxelles rue d'Aremberg 1791" show a large variety of popular styles. The factory closed in 1803.

Scandinavia

Denmark

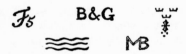

Although Denmark, Norway and Sweden had made faience very successfully for many years, they were slow to attempt the manufacture of porcelain. Several people with a knowledge of the manufacture of hard-paste porcelain apparently visited Denmark with a view to starting such a manufactory, but it was not until 1759 that a French modeller, Louis Fournier, came to Denmark at the invitation of King Frederick V, to produce the first Danish porcelain, a soft-paste porcelain. Probably because of its high cost, this factory closed in 1765 and consequently examples of this early factory are rare.

The quality of Fournier's paste varied, but in general it has a slight yellowish tinge and a rather dull glaze. The main output was apparently devoted to the production of table-wares which were decorated in the usual French styles of the period in a rather pale palette. The early mark was "F5" in blue enamel for Frederick V, and there is a solitary powder-box recorded with what is assumed to be the late mark of "C7", for Christian VII who succeeded Frederick in 1765.

Although china-clay was discovered on the island of Born-holm in 1755, it was not used until 1771 when F. H. Müller started producing porcelain and eventually established a factory there in 1775. The concern was taken over by the King in 1779.

A great deal of the success of the Copenhagen factory was due to the work of J. G. von Langen and A. C. Luplau, both of whom had previously worked at Fürstenberg, as director and modeller respectively. During the first quarter of the nine-teenth century production almost ceased, but the factory survived to become the important concern it still is today.

The hard-paste porcelain of Müller in the period 1775–79 was extremely modest, consisting mainly of a hard cold-grey body painted in underglaze-blue, purple or iron-red. The influence of Fürstenberg is especially noticeable in the many examples having reeding, gadrooning, Rococo scrolled panels and *osier*-pattern borders.

Following the King's take-over there was a very obvious change to Neo-classical styles, which can be most easily envisaged by imagining most of Wedgwood's stoneware shapes with rather inappropriate additions of full-relief garlands of flowers, or portrait-heads in black silhouette.

Any collectors visiting Rosenborg Castle in Copenhagen should not fail to see the unique "*Flora Danica* Service". This service consisting of 1,602 pieces, was originally started in 1789 for the Russian Empress Catherine II, but it was not finished until 1802 and remained in Copenhagen. The entire decoration is taken from the 1761 work of Oeder on Danish flora, the painter being J. C. Bayer of Nuremberg.

The figures produced at Copenhagen were often copied from pieces made at earlier Continental factories, especially Sèvres. Luplau himself is known to have produced a great many of the models used in a series of Norwegian peasants.

Biscuit porcelain figures and plaques in the style of the famous sculptor Bertel Thorwaldsen (*d.* 1844) are fairly common but were not produced until after 1867. It should also be noted that the mysterious word "Eneret", so often seen impressed into such pieces, simply means "Copyright". The popular mark of three wavy lines adopted in 1775 represents the three stretches of sea surrounding the country: the Sound, and the Great and Little Belts. This device is still used on modern pieces together with the full name of the factory.

Marieberg

Before it produced porcelain, Marieberg was famous for its faience. Porcelain was not made until Pierre Berthevin, who had previously been both at Mennecy and Copenhagen, took charge as manager in 1766. The soft-paste porcelain and decoration employed during Berthevin's direction is so like Mennecy that it would be difficult to separate the wares of the two concerns were it not for the different factory-marks. In 1769 Berthevin was succeeded by Henrik Sten and the beautiful soft-paste porcelain of the early period was replaced by an unpleasant chalky hybrid material. This in turn was abandoned in about 1777 in favour of a true hard-paste, but few pieces of any importance were produced in this material.

In 1782 the factory was purchased by Nordenstolpe of Rörstrand but only survived for six more years.

The usual marks on Marieberg porcelain are an incised "MB" in monogram for "MarieBerg" or the three crown and shield device taken from the arms of the Swedish royal house of Vasa.

Bibliography

Spanish Arts, Juan F. Riaño, South Kensington Museum, 1879.

Talavera Pottery, Alice Wilson Frothingham, Hispanic Society of America, 1944.

German Porcelain, W. B. Honey, Faber, 1947.

French Faience, A. Lane, Faber, 1948.

French Porcelain, W. B. Honey, Faber, 1950.

European Ceramic Art, W. B. Honey, Faber, 1952.

Italian Maiolica, B. Rackham, Faber, 1952.

Dresden China, W. B. Honey, Faber, 1954.

Italian Porcelain, A. Lane, Faber, 1954.

Eighteen Century German Porcelain, G. Savage, Rockcliffe, 1958.

Three Centuries of Swedish Pottery, Intro. by R. J. Charleston, Victoria and Albert Exhibition, 1959.

French Porcelain of the 18th Century, G. Savage, Barrie & Rockcliff, 1960.

Pocket-book of German Ceramic Marks, J. P. Cushion, Faber, 1961.

Continental Porcelain, R. Charles, Benn, 1964.

German Porcelain and Faience, S. Ducret, Oldbourne, 1962.

Pottery Through the Ages, G. Savage, Cassell, 1963.

Pocket-book of French and Italian Ceramic Marks, J. P. Cushion, Faber, 1965.

Handbook of Pottery and Porcelain Marks, J. P. Cushion, Faber, 3rd Ed., 1965.

World Ceramics, R. J. Charleston (Editor), Hamlyn, 1968.

Index

193